Peter, Do Not Be Afraid

Something Good Will Happen

PETER FILAKOURIDIS

ISBN 979-8-89112-445-5 (Paperback)
ISBN 979-8-89112-446-2 (Digital)

Covenant Books
11661 Hwy 707
Murrells Inlet, SC 29576
www.covenantbooks.com

To my wife, Mary, who faithfully has loved
me and served alongside me.

And to Emmanuel Marangakis, a fisher of men, who
showed true Christian love to me in words and deeds.

CONTENTS

INTRODUCTION

When I decided to write my biography, my first goal was for my children and grandchildren to know how miraculously God has worked in my life over the years, through the various trials, dangers, and miracles. But as I was going along, I was contacted by a minister of God from Katerini, Greece, George Kantartzis, who had heard my testimony in churches in Greece and asked to interview me, which was later published in the Christian magazine *The Voice of the Gospel*.

Brother George and I became very good friends, confessing our mutual love for God and as fellow believers. Speaking with him, he suggested that I continue writing my biography for a book to be published so that people will know that God does wonders and miracles, even today. He protects, heals, and, above all, saves for eternal life, to all who call on Him with faith.

This is what God has done and is doing with a strong hand, not only to me but also to other people I have met over the years. May the actual facts I mention in the following pages encourage and inspire many others because

Jesus Christ is the same yesterday and today
and forever. (Hebrews 13:8 NIV)

PART 1

EARLIEST MEMORIES IN CAIRO

The first memories that I have of my childhood in Cairo, Egypt, are when I was about three and a half years old. One night I woke up terrified of what was happening outside. My parents later told me that there was an Egyptian mob celebrating Ramadan in the streets shouting and banging on the windows and doors of our homes in Cairo's Shobra district as they walked down the street. The Egyptians fasted all day until midnight and then got up and woke everyone else up to eat all night until dawn. The shocking awakening was very dramatic for me, and I will remember it for the rest of my life. The noise and commotion came mainly from children banging on windows with long sticks, shouting "Allah Akbar," which means "God is great." This was the environment we lived in.

My sister Tota and I

I remember one day my uncle Vasilis Kalomiris, my mother's brother, came and kissed me with a lot of love and said goodbye to us because he was going to leave with his family for Brisbane, Australia. He would hold me and throw me high in the air and then catch me. I remember even seeing the dust at the top of the door! I would see him again many years later when I served in the merchant marine and my ship would stop there in Australia.

When I became four years old, I remembered more. I attended kindergarten at a private elementary school in Cairo, run by two single sisters. A servant would take us there by bus, or sometimes we would walk there, and my father would come and take us home. In kindergarten we also learned Arabic for an hour at the end of the day; it was probably a demand of the country. In the first grade, we were also taught French, so I learned three languages at this school where I stayed until the fourth grade.

When I was six years old, my father seriously considered moving our family to Greece, where we had relatives on the islands of Rhodes, Leros (where my father came from), and Kalymnos. My father's family name was Filakouris. Our distant relatives came from Asia Minor at the end of the eighteenth century.

MEMORIES OF EGYPT

My father (John) and mother (Helen) and
sisters Tota and Kati and me (Peter)

Overall, we were very happy in Egypt and had a strong Greek community. My parents attended church at the church of St. Anargirous in Cairo. They had five children: Tota, me, Kathy, Anastasia, and George. Before me was born another brother, Dimitrios, who died when he was about three months old. That's why my name is Peter-Dimitrios, in memory of their son who died. If a child dies, it is not easy to overcome it, especially for the mother. The signs of pain in my mother's heart—I saw it until the end of her life.

St. Anargirous Greek Church of Cairo

The Greeks in Egypt were very affluent. At that time two million people lived in Cairo, of whom 60,000–70,000 were Greeks. In Alexandria there were about 25,000 Greeks, while in Suez, Heliopolis, Ismailia, Port Said, and Port Fuad, about 40,000 ("Greece and the Mass Exodus of Egyptian Greeks, 1956–1966" by John Sakkas in the *Journal of Hellenic Diaspora*). Greeks have lived in Egypt since pre-Christian times, and they all preserved their faith, their traditions, and their language. Greece was only a short flight or two days away by boat. In Egypt, we were Greek citizens, and we paid a residence fee of one pound per person, so we paid seven pounds a year for a residence permit for the whole family.

There were many communities of foreigners there in Cairo: French, English, Jews, Italians, Americans, and Maltese. But lately Egyptians had become increasingly hostile to foreigners. One day my mother was on the bus, and while talking to a friend in Greek, an Egyptian woman yelled at them angrily and told them to speak in Arabic so that others would understand what they were talking about. The other Egyptian women laughed at my mother and her friend, and that made them very uncomfortable. My parents were fluent in Arabic, as well as three other languages. My mother was an excellent seamstress and worked in a workshop. This skill helped our family later immensely. In Egypt, we had everything we wanted and lived a comfortable life. My father worked for a very good salary at the Shell Oil Company in Cairo. He grew up without a father, and when he was about thirteen years old, an Armenian family friend took him to work to train him to become an engineer. Eventually, he became a Shell Company driver and drove huge trucks of oil to be loaded onto cargo ships waiting in port. At that time there were no oil pipelines.

I was six years old traveling to Greece for the first time.

In the summer of 1951, this is why we made a reconnaissance trip to Greece: there were great riots in Egypt against King Farouk and against the Coptics, the Greek Orthodox, the Armenians, and the Christians, which is why many suffered and died. My father and I went to Alexandria by train to board a ferry to Greece. By the 1950s, the political environment was becoming unstable for Europeans. So my father and I went to Rhodes to see if he could find a job and if there was the possibility for our whole family to move there permanently.

I remember very vividly the day we boarded the ship in Alexandria. I was wearing a sweater with red-and-blue stripes, and my father took a picture of me. I had a good time with my father. He loved our family very much and protected us many times from fanatical Egyptians when we were outside our home. But the Coptic Egyptians were good people and were very friendly to us. Something was beginning at that time among the Egyptians, which would later develop into war.

We arrived in Rhodes, and there we met Uncle Michael, the brother of Grandmother Kokona. He had a small lantern maintenance shop. A few days later after we arrived, he took us to a campsite in the mountains, where he was responsible for maintaining the generators of the camp Prophet Elisha. This place was created at the expense of the state for the poor children of the surrounding Greek islands, who could stay there for a month during their summer holidays. Every day all the children played soccer; many of these poor children came barefoot and were given three meals a day and some instructions. Later, when my family moved permanently to Rhodes and I was in fifth and sixth grade, I went to this camp myself!

We stayed in the cabins, and I hung out with the Greek children from the islands. These children were speaking bad words that I didn't know in Egypt. They were tougher than the Greek children I knew in Egypt. We stayed there for about a month and then returned to Egypt. My father started thinking seriously about moving to Rhodes and finding a job there. But then something happened that delayed this trip. My brother George, who was back in Cairo, grew very ill. He had rashes all over his body and a high fever. We had good doctors there, and they tried all kinds of medicine to cure him. For six months he remained ill, and we spent most of our savings going to private doctors. Thank God, he got well, but my father decided it wasn't time yet to move to Greece.

In the 1950s, the streets in Cairo were made of sandy dirt, and only the main roads were paved. It was then that the construction of cobbled roads began, using convict workers from prisons. Every twenty to thirty feet, there were soldiers with guns to supervise the workers to work and prevent escape. I could see the whole process from our balcony on the first floor. I also saw the soldiers beating the prisoners when they didn't work hard enough.

Every September and October, when the Nile River flooded and overflowed its banks, the water turned red. During these times, our whole family had tiny rashes on our backs because of an infectious disease called *hamonile*. I remember these rashes were so itchy that they bled from scratching and became infected. We suffered a lot every year from this disease. I can't remember it, but as my mother used to tell me, when I was about three years old, my whole head had pimples, which is why I had very weak hair all my life.

One day I saw a young girl die on the street in front of our apartment building! Some Egyptian children played with fire, lighting old newspapers with them. The little girl was running after them, and in an instant, she fell and a huge truck passed over her before my eyes! In half an hour, the police and her parents arrived, crying and screaming for the loss of their young daughter.

Our balcony in our house in Cairo

When the policemen caught thieves, they tied their hands behind their backs and made them walk to the station to charge them and all the time beat them on the back with bamboo sticks. Many women came to public fountains, filled their clay pots with clean water, balanced them on their heads, and left for their homes.

Camels, a special animal for the desert

Hundreds of camels passed by in front of our building and were probably going to the slaughterhouse. Very often one would stop to expel the water it drank, and then they would all stop and do the same. The camels drink about twenty gallons of water at a time, which is why the road became very muddy. The camel's meat, dark and lean, could be seen hanging from hooks in the meat market, while the liver would be about one meter long! My parents never bought camel meat for food.

How much I loved watching my mother light the fire on the stove! One day I picked up a match and lit it and was amazed at what I saw. Accidentally, however, the paper hanging from the shelves above the stove caught fire, which quickly spread throughout the kitchen! Eventually they extinguished it with water, but the destruction was too great. That night my father punished me very severely for causing such damage.

We didn't have a refrigerator, so we had to cook fresh food three times a day. We stored water in thin clay pots on the shelf next to the window, which we left a little open, to let air in to cool the kitchen and the food left outside, as well as the clay pots with water. In the evening we had a lot of cockroaches, three to four centimeters long!

Grandma and Grandpa Nicolaides

I remember, when I was seven to eight years old, I went to visit my grandparents, alone, in the village of Zetun. The journey took about twenty-five minutes and was still quite safe at the time. A servant took me to the train station. I took my ticket and showed it to the train conductor. Because I was traveling alone, I had to count five stops and then get off and walk for three to four minutes, until I reached their house. The train was passing by King Farouk's palace before my stop. There were no cars then, only carts on the sandy roads.

Breakfast trolley with rice and lentils

In front of our home in Cairo, street vendors were passing by, carrying breakfast food on trolleys or carts. The food was a large pile of cooked rice called *koshari*, along with lentils, while under the cart there was a lamp to keep the food warm. I really wished I had some of it, but my parents wouldn't let us eat from street vendors for hygiene reasons. They put the rice in a mug and sold it to street workers. After eating it, they took the mug, rinsed it in a basin of water, and used it again for the next customer. Another cart had *ful mudammas* rice and large beans. *Belila* was another food made from cooked wheat boiled with milk and sugar, which was left overnight and sold for breakfast as well.

Licorice drink they sold on the street; a happy salesman

On the street they sold a drink called *arlisoos*. It was licorice-flavored water. They filled a cup from a copper container, and after the customer drank it, they rinsed it in a basin of dirty water. I wish I could have had a little, but Mom wouldn't let me.

Next to us lived a man who was a polisher of bronze vases and pots. He had four wives who helped him in this work. They smeared the vessels with a metal cream and rubbed them everywhere with force, and after a cleansing process, they shone like new. If they didn't do their job well, at night he would beat them, and we could hear them screaming while he kept beating them. I didn't like this man at all.

Whenever there was a funeral or wedding, they would come and set up a huge tent in the middle of the road, so the cars had to go around the tent. They put canvases to fence off the stage, laid a cloth on the floor, and brought in food and drink, and at weddings they danced in there. I remember the soldiers playing wrestling with huge sticks, and then the belly dancers continued the entertainment. At funerals, women painted their faces and eyes with henna, a dark dye. They screamed for a long time, pulling their hair, and this was done at very lavish funerals. These women were paid to cry at funerals.

Large sails to catch even the slightest blow of wind

My father often took us to Rod El Farak for food and drink, next to the Nile River. Most Europeans went there because the environment was clean and cared for. There were also sailing boats there, for the wealthy Egyptians, who wanted to relax by cruising on the Nile. The larger the boat, the more family members could board. The boats had huge sails because the winds were weak in the usually calm waters of the Nile.

SOME MORE MEMORIES
FROM EGYPT

I also won't forget the locust raid that took place in Cairo in 1951 or '52. Their swarms were so numerous that they covered the sky! We got out of school, and locust were falling on us like rain. They were green and ten centimeters long. Within hours on the ground was a layer of locust about six inches deep covering the schoolyard! We walked by stepping on them, and they climbed on our feet! Fortunately, our parents soon came and took us home.

I often listened to Greek songs from Athens on the radio. After the news from Athens, we heard news from the island Cyprus, which encouraged the freedom fighters (EOKA) with speeches and patriotic songs against the English occupiers. My grandparents were once invited to a feast organized by King Farouk in Cairo. He had invited the Europeans of the region. The requirements to attend was to have clothes made for you to wear and measurements would be taken for the clothes and even special shoes to be worn at the feast. My grandparents thought this was too much and didn't go after all, but they greatly appreciated the invitation of the king.

From the movie *The Ten Commandments*

During this time, they were shooting the movie *The Ten Commandments* by Cecil DeMille in the Cairo desert. My grandparents were invited and took part in the film as extras. For the purposes of the film, they had built an entire city on the sands of the desert. My grandparents were given one British pound a day to wear clothes and sandals and walk in the desert among the crowds.

When I was at school in Cairo in fourth or fifth grade, I put on my white shirt and short white pants one day, and I was getting ready to go for a math exam at school. I sharpened my pencil with my father's double-edged old-fashioned shaving blade. I was only to wear these white clothes on Sundays, but I wanted to wear them for my math exam. But when my father came and saw me, he got very angry and raised his hand to hit me. I was then frightened. I brought my hands to my face, forgetting that I was holding the blade. As a result, I cut my forehead very badly over my right eye! My mother came in screaming because she thought I had cut off my eye. They rushed me to the hospital, where they sewed up my cut, and then took me to school, after changing clothes, because the ones I was wearing were bloodied. From this event, a scar can be seen on my forehead to this day.

My sisters wore blue skirts and white blouses to school, and on Sunday they wore white skirts and blouses. School buses took us to church as well as to school. Years later, when we were in Greece, we could wear any clothing, but we would always have to wear a school hat with an anchor and an owl on it, to indicate the school we were going to. All the boys of the island had to wear their hats everywhere, wherever they went, day or night.

My father later found a good job in Attaka, northeast of Suez. The owners of this work were Jewish. He became the supervisor to oversee the dynamite explosions of the mountain, the loading of the rocks onto trucks, and the maintenance of all machinery involved. These trucks carried the rocks to the barges for the maintenance of the Suez Canal.

Often, the Shell Oil Company sent my father to the Sinai Peninsula to repair trucks and buses of St. Catherine's Monastery. Scientists, theologians, and tourists visited the area and did various research and studies. They were the ones who told him about what was inside the monastery and about some rare ancient manuscripts that were kept there.

Monastery of St. Catherine in Sinai

Meanwhile, fear and problems were growing in Egypt's Greek community. Many Greeks began to move to Greece, Australia, and Canada and transfer their money to Swiss banks. I had started fifth grade when all this turmoil was going on in the country.

The Suez Canal was built in 1866 by Ferdinand de Lesseps, a French architect and diplomat. He tried to build the Panama Canal but was unsuccessful due to mosquitoes causing malaria and killing hundreds of workers, so he abandoned the attempt, leaving the Americans to complete the project. He then moved to Egypt to complete the Suez Canal, creating an artificial passage to the

Mediterranean Sea so that ships would not travel around Africa to reach Europe and avoid Cape Town storms. Thus, large vessels using the canal had to pay a large sum of money to the French government to pass through the canal. The plan was to give the canal to Egypt after a hundred years of use and compensation for its construction costs.

My father decided to work in those granite mountains that would be used in the Suez Canal to hold back the banks and prevent soil erosion. He worked from morning till night. He was responsible for the explosions, loading, and transportation of broken rocks by American and English truck drivers. He stayed there for a year and liked the area so much that we all moved from Cairo to Suez around August 1956. Very few families lived there. Many Greeks worked there as barge workers and rock sorters. The Jewish company gave us a huge house with servants and a chicken coop with chickens, pigeons, and ducks. I remember going fishing with my father and grandfather and catching fish using only a bucket. Due to the tide, the sea level sometimes rose and sometimes receded, and the water was warm and very salty. In August 1956 we moved there. I started the fifth grade in a Greek school in Suez. They made fun of me and called me "the capital" because those who came from the capital were rich and seemed to "know it all." We had a great time as a family, swimming in the Suez sea.

We had a huge female dog named Garia. In town, there were trained dogs defending the small town from wild wolves, who sometimes entered the city to attack. Garia came to my father one day and, grabbing him by the leg, pulled him outside by his pants and stopped by a hole in the ground. Then Garia went down inside the hole and came out one by one with ten little puppies! After this, my parents gave her extra food for her babies.

When the sea receded, we searched for holes in the rocky bottom, and inside we found fish and crabs. When there was a full moon, we caught very fat crabs. One time my grandfather and grandmother came from Cairo and visited us. While they were visiting us, my father decided to go fishing. We boarded a rusty metal rowboat and moved away about three hundred meters from the shore to go fishing.

They warned us not to go too far because the afternoon winds would start blowing toward the deep sea. We started around 10:00 a.m. We caught so many fish! How much fun we had! It was a hot day, and the winds started blowing toward the deep sea. Then my father and grandfather started rowing for us to return to shore, but the boat kept moving away from the shore! I was so thirsty that I drank salt water, causing me to sweat, while my head felt like it was going to burst! Fortunately, at that time a motorboat passed by and pulled us back to shore. I jumped off the boat and ran home. I poured plenty of cool water on my head and drank as much as I could! We had blisters from our long stay in the sun. I will not forget the thirst and heat I felt on that metal boat. I thought I was going to die!

A rusty metal boat

A bit of history

The Suez Canal, as I mentioned earlier, was designed and completed by Ferdinand de Lesseps. The canal would significantly shorten the long journey around Africa's southernmost cape because ships would only need two to three days to cross it and reach the Mediterranean Sea. By law, the French would have given the channel to Egypt in 1966, but Gamal Abdel Nasser wanted to get it ten years earlier, breaking the agreement with the French government.

And a bit of politics

Egypt had a general, President Mohamed Naguib, who was pro-European. They were all dictators. Everything was going well with him, and he had even asked US President Eisenhower for financial help repairing the Aswan Dam, which controlled the flow of water coming from the vast lakes of Victoria, Tanganyika, and Nyasa in Central Africa. All the dirty water from these lakes ended up in the Nile, which, when overflowing, caused damage to farms, homes, and cities; so it needed to be controlled, which was done with the construction of the dam. Life developed around the river on both sides in an arid desert. Herodotus, an ancient Greek historian, called Egypt "a gift of the Nile."

Khrushchev, Russia's president, agreed to give financial aid to Egypt, but not to President Naguib but to Gamal Abdel Nasser. Thus, President Naguib disappeared from the political scene and Egypt, took money from Russia to repair the dam. Khrushchev also sent "advisers" to Egypt, and Nasser nationalized everything in the country: private property, banks, business, and so forth.

Russia wanted only one thing from Egypt: to turn against Europe and America. Egypt had helped Israel and Europe for many years. In the Bible, in the book of Genesis in chapter 12, God states that whoever blesses Israel is blessed, and whoever curses Israel is cursed. The seed of Abraham is Jesus Christ, and those who honor and follow Him will be blessed forever. However, Gamal Abdel Nasser, now Prime Minister of Egypt, did not want to wait another ten years, so in September 1956, he placed the Suez Canal under Egyptian control.

Back in 1951 when we lived in Cairo, there was an uprising against Christians, Armenians, and Coptics by Muslims, and they killed many, including entire Coptic families in Egypt. One day our neighbor showed us some writing on the front wall of our building, and my mother went out to see. There were seven crosses painted with chalk on the wall. My mother immediately took a piece of cloth and cleaner and removed the crosses. They represented the seven Christians in our family who lived inside! The next day we heard about horrific deaths of families throughout the neighborhood. Innocent people were killed, and we believe it was what my mother did that saved our family's life that night.

And then came troubles

When we were at the Greek school in Suez in October 1956, I was in fifth grade. We heard gun noises in the distance. The Israeli army was fighting the Egyptians in the nearby desert. Trucks of the Egyptian army came and took us home away from this battle. There was confusion as to where to take us, so my sisters and I told them we were from the Attaka area, and they took us there. Meanwhile, my parents had come to the school to pick us up, but they couldn't find us. Later that night they came and found us safe and sound in the house in Attaka. The situation was then tense and dangerous for everyone near the Suez Canal.

The Attaka mountains in the distance, near Suez

> Then they cried to the Lord in their trouble,
> and he saved them from their distress.
> He brought them out of darkness, the utter
> darkness, and broke away their chains. (Psalms
> 107:13–14 NIV)

Our home in Attaka was closer to the battlefield, so in the evenings we could hear the noise of guns and see flashes in the night sky. We were told to leave the area quickly, so the trucks of the Egyptian army took us again to the city of Suez for safety because "the Israelis were coming." We left the servants behind along with a lot of property. We stayed at a Greek friend's house for a week there in the city of Suez. We had a lot of friends in town. The Egyptian army offered weapons to untrained civilians, including my father, in case the Israelis attacked Suez. My father refused to take a gun because that would give the Israelis another reason to kill us. My mother didn't want my father to take up arms either because Israelis, she said, are God's people.

When we were in Suez, we heard that Israeli soldiers were conducting air strikes over the desert, about ten kilometers outside the city, and were dropping parachuters in the middle of the night. The Egyptians found out, and they all left the city they were hiding in and went out into the desert to kill the paratroopers as they descended, which goes against the rules of engagement in war. To their surprise, they found that these paratroopers were just dummies for bait, while in the meantime, Israeli soldiers had parachuted near the city in jeeps. They moved into the desert, found the Egyptians, surrounded them, and took them as prisoners. The next day a photo in the newspaper showed young Israeli soldiers with their machine guns guarding hundreds of Egyptians. We even heard and saw Israeli planes flying over the city so close to the high-rise buildings that they were breaking the windows from the pressure of their engines!

The French flew their warplanes, hitting airfields in Port Said, Port Suez, and Heliopolis near Cairo. My uncle, Kostas Triantafyllou, was working as a gasoline supplier to the Caltex company at the airport and was shot in the arm during this battle. He almost lost his arm! Years later, in July 1975, my wife and I saw him in Athens and stayed with them for a day or two. He showed us the scar on his left arm, as well as the four-inch bullet, which was removed from his arm.

After two weeks, the fighting ceased, and the English ships left Port Said, leaving the port to the Egyptians. All this was a lesson for them because President Nasser had illegally taken control of the Suez Canal.

Just before we left the area, my father and I returned to our home in Attaka to collect various last-minute things and take them with us to Greece. A very unpleasant surprise awaited us when we got to our home. We had hoped to see our beautiful house with furnished rooms, servants cleaning, banana and palm trees in the yard, and a fishing boat, but how shocked we were when we saw none of this. It took us four to five hours to reach the Attaka area from Cairo. We had a kitchen, a bathroom inside the house and one outside, a bird cage, servants, a beautiful Persian carpet in the middle of the living room, and a dining table with chairs. Our plan was to take some clothes for my mother and sisters, while some other things we would give to our neighbors. Unfortunately, when we entered our house, there was nothing to take. How disappointed we were! We went inside and saw that the Egyptian soldiers had broken the table and used it for firewood in the middle of the carpet to boil water and make tea! They must have been uncouth peasants who had not lived in the city. We had lamps and stoves in the kitchen, but they lit wood in the middle of the living room to make tea! All wardrobes were empty; silverware, clocks, and other furniture had disappeared. The cage in the house was open, and all the birds were gone. I believe the soldiers simply wanted to destroy our property out of hatred for foreigners. We left very disappointed. We found many of our old Egyptian neighbors, who were also very sorry for what the Egyptian soldiers had done to our house. So we left with nothing. We took an empty suitcase back to Cairo.

After that, we went to my grandparents' house in Cairo, from November to January, until the government told us to leave Egypt. They gave us the choice of either becoming Egyptian citizens or leaving the country as Greek citizens. My father rejected the Egyptian citizen's choice because he did not want him or his sons to fight against the Israeli army in any future wars.

In January, we went to the port in Alexandria, where the ship would take us to Greece where we would go to stay with relatives there. Alexandria was a Greek city built by Alexander the Great.

Greek culture prevailed throughout the region for more than two thousand years. In Alexandria, we lived with Mr. Roupailiotis, a cousin of my mother, for a week, while we waited for the ship to arrive. Father signed a paper that stated all our rights and property would be given to the Egyptian government. So we left Egypt with one suitcase for each person. Then we learned that nothing is more precious than life itself, so we left with nothing, without food, and with little money. We wore our best and warmest clothes because it was winter in Greece and it was very cold. We were very concerned about our safety. I was eleven years old at the time, Tota sixteen, Kathi nine, Anastasia seven, and George five.

> They were glad when it grew calm, and
> he guided them to their desired haven. (Psalm
> 107:30 NIV)

At the port in Alexandria, waiting for the ship, I saw hundreds of thousands of refugees boarding the ships every day. I saw things that didn't make sense to an eleven-year-old. I saw Greeks and Jews being pushed into the rooms by brutal young Egyptian soldiers with machine guns, who were inspecting them and grabbing their clothes. Many Jewish women hid diamonds in their bodies, and soldiers forcibly searched for them. My father was strong and could fight with any of them, but then we would have another hundred against us and they would punish us all. A young soldier with dirty fingers pushed my father because he didn't want us to speak Greek but only Arabic. My father told him, "Since you only speak Arabic, we will only speak Greek," and this made the soldier angry. How I wanted to kick this soldier, but I didn't! I kept my composure out of fear. It was very hard to hear the women screaming and seeing crowds of people in distress, as well as the sudden gunfire in the air. It was shocking.

The Greek officers of the ship were angry about the way the soldiers treated the Greeks on the dock, and coming down from the ramp, they told the soldiers not to disturb the Greeks, who were not to blame for anything, and then they separated us from the rest, putting us first on the ship. The Egyptians hated the Jews, the French, and the English. The Greeks had a good reputation in Egypt before the crisis, but how can you explain this to disorganized, rude, and ignorant Egyptian soldiers? Our biggest problem was that we were kicked out with a group of Jews, just because my father worked for a Jewish company, so we were treated badly as the Jews were.

The Egyptian government had told us to leave as soon as possible because we were foreigners. I didn't see anyone killed or shot, but I saw many young soldiers pushing the crowds down into the harbor with their guns. Finally, we boarded the Greek ship *Lydia* and ran to find a place to sit on deck. On the ship they gave us some blankets from the Greek army, to protect us from the cold winter. I remember my father gave me five drachmas after exchanging some money on the boat. There was no food to buy, nor did we bring any with us, but they gave us some sandwiches on board the ship. It was so wonderful to hear Greeks on the ship talking, without anyone screaming, and we finally calmed down from the chaos in the port of Alexandria. We traveled two days, and in the morning of the third day, we arrived at the port of Piraeus. We had only a few British pounds left since we paid for our trip on the boat and then had to go to the island of Rhodes, where our relatives were waiting for us.

In the port of Piraeus near Athens, Greece, we waited to board a ship to go to Rhodes but found out that we had to wait a couple of days before one came, so we stayed in a cheap hotel with a name Kalymnos, the island of sponge divers. We paid ten drachmas for a room. We went out with my mother and sisters to buy sandwiches, and while walking down the street, we saw bad girls and boys with very bad behavior and learned that this area had a very bad reputation. We heard shouting and fighting all night, so we left after two days. On the way out, we saw sailors and soldiers with these girls, cursing with such bad words that I had never heard in my life.

I know now after traveling around the world years later that nowhere have I heard worse language against God than in Greece. Sadly, I say that God will judge those who curse Him, of course if they do not repent. How can they utter such filthy and horrible words against the Creator of the universe, who will one day judge the world according to His righteousness, and who gave His beloved only-begotten Son to die on the cross for our sins? Yes, He loves us so much. He is a God of love, but also a god of justice and judgment. How can people say they are Christians and curse the very god they say they believe? Whoever confesses his sins, repents, and believes in the Lord Jesus Christ will be saved. These things I pondered in my heart.

> The Lord will keep you from all harm—he
> will watch over your life. (Psalm 121:7 NIV)

Last photo of the family, before we left Egypt

RHODES, THE FINAL DESTINATION

When we finally arrived in Rhodes (the "promised land"), we were surprised by the poverty that prevailed there. My uncle, Michael Kouravelis, had a shop in the area of Agios Ioannis, where he repaired gas stoves. These gas canisters operated on kerosene. Repeatedly pressing a valve to the side increased the pressure, and you could ignite a strong enough flame for cooking food. But instead of kerosene, they used dirty oil from trucks, so the valves became clogged over time. My uncle's job was to clean these blocked valves. He received about fifty drachmas a day, which was a good amount at the time, enough to support his family, but not an extra family of seven. My uncle's son was a lawyer and worked as a justice of the peace on the island of Symi.

Need for an apartment

Old houses with cobbled streets in the castle of Rhodes, in the old town

My uncle, looking for a room for us to rent, went to the castle area. There were the cheapest houses in the city that were centuries old. You could paint the stone walls internally, but without any further intervention in the construction. The exterior had to look old. Eventually, he found us a room upstairs in a house, where seven to eight families lived in many other rooms, and we paid a hundred drachmas for rent for a month.

One bathroom was outside and was common to all families. Those who had a job, if lucky, made thirty to fifty drachmas a day. The next step was for my father to find a job. Until that happened, my parents were forced to give their wedding rings to a pawnshop for three hundred drachmas. This money covered two months' rent and some food expenses. In addition to some blankets we had, Uncle gave us a wooden table he made, a bench, some lanterns, a few pots, two chairs, a bucket, and a few towels. It was a very cold winter, and we slept on the floor. Our uncle gave us more blankets. To keep warm, we slept next to each other, and yet we all said we were so happy now. Thank God! What happiness we live in now! There was no longer a ship, no soldiers, no one who spoke Arabic! Thank God, we are in our country and everyone loves us. We were poor and safe.

We had no water, so we took an empty, five-gallon square bucket that had contained feta cheese from my uncle and nailed a broomstick to one side for a handle. I was ashamed to go and fetch water with the bucket, so Tota went during the specific hours when the water supply was available in the area. The common latrine was outside the house where we were staying and had a cardboard door. In the morning, we waited in line to use it. Many brought the bucket they used during the night from their room and emptied it into the latrine hole. To rinse the bucket, we waited for Tota to fetch water. There were seven of us in my family, and there was only one latrine for about twenty-five people!

There was a soup kitchen in town for the poor, a few blocks away. Our uncle put us on the soup kitchen list to receive about one gallon of soup each day per family. The soup sometimes had meat leftovers from restaurants and a bit of red color. City hall officials helped the poor in this way, along with half a loaf of bread every day.

House of Mercy—where food was given to the poor

My brother George and I at the restaurant House of Mercy (2019)

My uncle got us a voucher from the town hall, with which we could take food as refugees. The Greeks on the islands, but also in all parts of Greece, expected this to happen because of the war and were ready to help the Greeks from Egypt as much as they could. The richest refugees went to Athens and stayed there. We were the poorest of all, so we went to the island to survive. What could be worse than that? Well, wait and I'll tell you what did happen a few days later. However—I will admit it—God was and had always been with us. We met some friends and especially a very good lady who liked us and helped us. I was a young boy growing up, and I ate everything I could find, but I always felt very hungry. We ate only half of our soup and some of our bread at noon and kept the rest until nightfall. We stayed there in the castle a month. One day, while walking down the street, I found a puppy and took him home. "Are you crazy?" my father said to me. "What are we going to feed it, since we have no food?" With a gray little puppy, I was the happiest boy in the world. So happy, I didn't know how miserable I was!

The house we were staying in was an old Turkish house located in the castle walls and had a balcony. Every year they took clay (*patelia*) from the mountains and covered the roof. Thus, year after year, the thickness of the roof reached half a meter, while the wooden beams below were bent by the heavy weight of the roof. There were already many tons of clay on the roof; however, during the winter, they climbed to the roof from a wooden staircase and laid a new layer of clay. It had been like this for many years, so we didn't see any risk of collapse, although there were definite signs.

Then something unprecedented happened to us, which was very scary! Just when our lives couldn't get any worse, disaster struck! An earthquake, on February 19, 1957. I remind you that we lived all our lives in Egypt and never had an earthquake, so when we heard the hum and saw the houses collapse in the middle of that rainy, cold winter night, we didn't know what was happening. A huge volume of clay, about half a square meter, fell from the ceiling, right next to sister Kathi's head, while we were all sleeping on the floor! From the fall a hole opened in our floor, which continued further down to the first floor, where there was a young couple with a child, who survived with no injury. All the occupants of the building were screaming and running in panic to get out into the street, coming down a steep staircase. We all ran barefoot in pajamas on the wet road in the rain. The earthquake was very strong and lasted a long time. Many houses were destroyed, and some people were killed. It was felt on other islands as well. We ran and found shelter along the castle wall, which protected us somewhat from the rain and the icy wind.

The high wall of the castle did not fall. Police were riding bicycles around the area to check the situation and see if there were any serious injuries. We were not seriously hurt, except for some scratches on our knees, arms, and legs because we were running over the stones and debris that had fallen on the cobbled roads. It was a miracle that none of us were seriously injured. God had saved my sister's life as well as ours. Now I know why we were saved. God's hand was upon us, and I learned it later by reading verse 14 from the apostle Paul's

Epistle to the Hebrews, chapter 1: *"Are not all angels ministering spirits sent to serve those who will inherit salvation?"* (This means that God sees ahead of time those who love Him and He protects them with angels.)

We became refugees and were saved from certain death. God brought us out of misery, away from Islamic hatred, away from weapons and soldiers, Muslims and dictators in Egypt. We had reached the brink of destruction, but He put His hand on us and grabbed us, saving our lives. My parents were crying, and I remember my mother saying to my father, "John, at least we were saved!" Things got worse, but that story will continue later.

Many earthquake victims went to stay at their relatives' homes, but we had nowhere to go. The whole area was full of stones and debris. At last, it dawned and the nightmare of the night ended at the first light of day. A good lady brought us some food. Then we went to another area, away from the rain. We stayed there all day and all night in the cold winter. My father and I went to the front gate of the castle (Agios Georgios), where cars were passing by, and they were giving out some money (small coins), blankets, and cans of food for the earthquake victims. I remember a high priest passed by in a black limousine with his driver, who lowered the window, blessed us with a gesture, and left! My father was very angry with him for the indifference he showed. However, that good lady, who helped us the first time, came again the next day and brought us some soup and a loaf of bread.

> Then they cried out to the Lord in their trouble, and he delivered them from their distress. (Psalm 107:6 NIV)

Around 3:00–4:00 p.m. on the third day, a man came by and asked why we didn't go to a house. He spoke in broken Greek to my father and invited us to go to his house, which was nearby, to accommodate us. He was a teacher at the local Turkish high school. How very happy we were! We ran to his house. My brother George was about six years old, Tota fifteen, Kathi ten, and Anastasia eight.

He had a very nice, cozy house with two bedrooms. Their bed was given to my parents while they slept on the floor! We, along with their children, would sleep on the floor, in the other room. This good man did the right thing, while thousands of others passed by and did nothing for us! This work of kindness remained forever etched in my heart. To this day, I remember this gift of kindness with tears in my eyes. Remember this event. Something amazing happens to me years later to allow me to thank him.

We stayed about a week with them, until the Department of the Interior (from the King's Provision), along with America's Sixth Fleet, gave us a tent, food, and blankets. We left their warm house and stayed in the tent somewhere nearby but within the castle walls. A huge bamboo pole held the tent up. The blankets on the floor were now paradise for us! We got a gallon of soup every day and two loaves of black bread from the soup kitchen. This delicious soup was made of boiled tomatoes, spaghetti, and spices.

The castle wall opposite our tent   The area where our tent was located

South entrance of the castle near our tent

Enlarge the place of your tent, stretch your tent curtains wide, do not hold back; lengthen your cords, strengthen your stakes. (Isaiah 54:2 NIV)

Then we had to share our tent with another family of three because they ran out of tents to be provided to the public. The names in this family were Vouli, Evdokia, and Michalis. (I remember those names, even though over sixty years have passed!) So we stayed in the other half of the tent, seven people in a space of about ten square meters! My father lifted the tent up higher off the ground so that we could stick our feet out when we lay down. We spent a few months in this tent. It was so miserable, yet we were happy. We played hide-and-seek, marbles, and soccer with all the other children in the area.

I call on the Lord in my distress, and he answers me. (Psalm 120:1 NIV)

One day I complained to God that we were hungry and wanted eggs fried in olive oil. We were playing around the houses that had been destroyed. Several chickens were running around, and we wanted to catch one to slaughter them for meat, but Father wouldn't let us because they weren't ours. Mom said, "God will provide." We took leftovers of food from nearby restaurants, as well as some other food brought to us every day by a woman who worked there and kept them for us before washing the dishes. We ate everything with such appetite that we didn't even leave a bone!

A great food discovery

One afternoon we were playing hide-and-seek, and as I crouched under a bush, I found a bunch of eggs in a hole! I came out and told everyone to stop playing and that it was time to leave. After a while I went back to that hole and carefully took out all the eggs and brought them home to our tent. We kept them in a cool place, and every morning, Mom broke them one by one, and if they were okay, then we had fried eggs for breakfast! We threw away some of them because they were broken or spoiled. The chickens kept going there and laying eggs, so we had fresh eggs for our family.

> Surely the arm of the Lord is not too short
> to save, nor his ear too dull to hear. (Isaiah 59:1
> NIV)

My father's profession was mechanical engineering. After much searching, he was finally hired in a Turkish blacksmith shop. His job was to sharpen sharp metals with a file all day.

Something I was very ashamed to do was go to a public fountain in the square and get water for our family. Everyone filled their buckets daily for the necessary drinking water, but also for cleaning purposes. At the time, I was still in fifth grade. My other siblings also continued school, except for Tota, who stayed home, that is, in the tent, substituting for our mother, who went to town working as a seamstress. Thus, Tota would take care of cleaning, shopping, and cooking. She would put a couple of stones around the stove to cut down the wind and cook there. Grandpa and Grandma were still in Egypt because they had some problems with the government. Eventually they came to Rhodes, but they went to a village on the west side of the island and stayed in a room they rented there.

Our kerosine cooking stove

When we lived in the tent, not everything was nice, not only because we had to share the space with another family but because we had another very serious problem. The stakes supporting the tent were made of bamboo. Over time we learned that bedbugs had hidden in them and at night came out and stung us. These parasitic insects sucked blood out of our legs and stomachs and arms. The more blood they sucked, the bigger they grew. To exterminate them, we squeezed them, but they gave off a disgusting smell like a sewer! We found them hidden everywhere: in the corners of the tent, on the edges of our pillows, in the bamboo poles. We killed them with kerosene, which is why our tent smelled of kerosene and stunk horribly for many days.

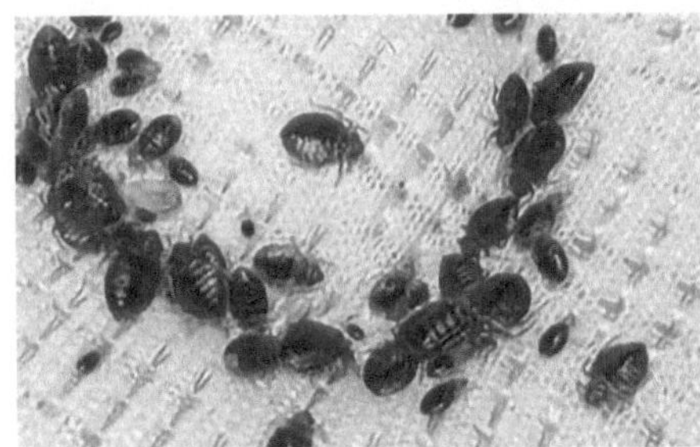

Happy bedbug family

Typical tents

There is a beginning of new changes for good

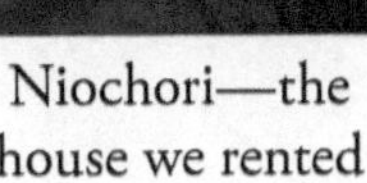

Niochori—the
house we rented

Rhodes, 1958

Little by little, we managed to raise enough money and started looking for a house to rent. Finally, we found ourselves in Niochori, near the beach. It was a very strange, two-story house, which had a room on each floor. The kitchen and bathroom were on the ground floor.

We lived in this area for three years. My siblings and I walked about three kilometers to go to elementary school and later high school. We all walked to school for economic reasons. We couldn't afford bus fare for all of us every day, and we had no car. We passed through fields full of red poppies and later with white chamomile. All of us walked to school except for Tota, who took care of the house from the age of sixteen and no longer went to school.

CAMPING ON MT. PROPHET ELISHA

In fifth and sixth grade, I went for one month in the summer to a camp on the mountain of Prophet Elisha in Rhodes. It was the same camp I had visited with my father when I was six years old. In two two-story buildings, there were cabins with beds in rows and showers with cold water. The name of my cabin was Macedonia. Every morning we stood outside in rows in front of the flag, and after saying the Lord's Prayer, each cabin sang our theme song. Whichever cabin sang the loudest won. The theme for my cabin was

> Macedonia, Macedonia, I always have a wish,
> here it is, Macedonia, always Greek!

We started each day in a competitive spirit. They taught us to keep our beds made well, our clothes clean and tidy, and to help everyone to keep the camp in good condition. We loved exploring the area around the camp. At the back of the buildings stretched a ravine, and down low, there was a stream with running water. The slopes of the ravine were full of sage bushes and old German helmets. Some of them were rusty, while others were in good condition. We put them on and went back to the camp, but they wouldn't let us keep them, so we threw them back into the ravine.

My uncle Michalis would come there and maintain the electric generator so that the camp would have electricity. Every day a truck went down to the city of Rhodes and brought back fresh produce for our food. The greatest blessing there was the food! For breakfast we had eggs and rustic bread with butter and jam, at ten in the morning we ate fruit and again sliced bread with butter and jam, and at noon we had normal Greek casserole dishes. This was followed by speeches under the pines from twelve to one thirty, and then rest and sleep in the cabins from two to three in the afternoon. We ate bread, butter, and jam again and then played soccer in the fields with children from the other cabins. At 5:00 p.m., we had dinner and another talk. At 8:00 to 8:30 p.m., we went to our cabins to sleep. At 9:00 p.m., my uncle Michael would turn off the lights by shutting off the generator, and it was dark everywhere until morning. Of all the speeches they made for us, I don't remember any. But I'm sure they were good speeches.

The whole mountain was full of pine trees with pine cones. I collected thousands of pine nuts and ate them. We weren't allowed to climb trees, but I did it secretly. Years later, in 1975, my wife and I went to this area on a motorcycle and climbed the pines again, to show her how I did it back then, when I was a child. In the camp area there were many deer and squirrels. On Sundays we had to walk two or three kilometers to the church of Prophet Elisha there on the mountain. One Sunday, after the service, we had some free time before going back to the camp, and walking there around the church with some friends, we went down to a very deep basement with a rusty metal gate that read, "Don't enter." My friends and I read it as "Please enter." We opened it a little, and entering inside, we found another old wooden door and opened it timidly. The light slipped in, and out of the damp room came such a horrible smell that almost made me faint! On the floor there was a large pile of skulls and bones, while others had rolled and were scattered around. We stayed a few seconds motionless and shocked, then hurriedly left, closing the doors behind us. We will never forget that disgusting smell and what we saw that day! We later learned that these were bones from the cemetery that were dug up after twenty years of burial to make room for more bodies to be buried in the same spot. They do this process to this day.

There were many children in the camp, around two hundred to three hundred at a time. Most of them were poorer than us and came from the Dodecanese (the twelve islands on the east side of

Greece next to Turkey). They came to the camp wearing only a shirt, shorts, and no shoes. They ran in the fields on stones and thorns and did not get hurt because the skin on their feet had become as hard as a shoe sole! They were tough, strong players, and we couldn't beat them. They came from the islands of Symi and Kalymnos. When our month at camp ended, I felt sad and miserable. Going back to the city and the misery of poverty was almost unbearable for me. Next month my sisters would go to the girls' camp.

However, we had very good memories of our life there in Rhodes all these years. My sisters went to the city's girls' high school. I attended the boys' high school for three years, and because at that time there were not many engineering graduates, captains, and wireless radio officers of the merchant navy from the University of Athens, they passed a law where one could go from the third grade of high school directly to engineering school, after passing some special exams. So I took a few extra math and physics classes during the summer of 1960 and eventually passed all the exams and entered the engineering school at age fifteen!

I remember with little shame, while looking for adventure when I was in high school, we would sneak out of class an hour early, pretending we were sick with a headache or stomachache. The professor gave us permission to go home. But we went down the hill to the castle and climbed the walls, and through an opening, we entered the rooms that remained untouched there for centuries. The Crusaders had passed through this castle on their way to Jerusalem and on their way back to northern Europe. Some of the rooms had about five centimeters of dust with no trace of footprints on the floor. We were afraid of stepping on any skeletons! We didn't find swords or knives, but we loved the adventure.

My grandfather and grandmother had come from Egypt by now and lived in the village of Ixia in Rhodes on the west side of the island, about five to six kilometers away from the city. To visit them, they would give me five drachmas for the bus ticket, to go and return. They loved me very much. I had the name of my grandmother's brother, who died of tuberculosis in Cairo. I didn't take the bus because I wanted to keep the five drachmas for me. So, to get to their house, I would climb over Admiral Smith's Mountain (Mont de Smith), where the ancient stadium is located, and then descend the hill on the other side by climbing down rocks, bushes, and trees; and I would run to their house, trying to cover the distance in half an hour, to get there before the bus. I never told them I was doing that because I could buy five chocolates with that money! Sometimes I stayed for the weekend and sometimes a whole month during the summer. I was about thirteen or fourteen years old at the time.

During the summer months, on Sunday afternoons, I used to go to the Nautical Club of Rhodes, located at the entrance of the port of Mandraki. Rowing boat races were held at this club. The crew of the boat in which I participated consisted of four rowers and a helmsman. We did two to three hours of training and rowing, and then we competed with the others. We had to have a certain weight and strength to participate. This was going on all summer. The boats were made of polished walnut wood with rolling and moving seats. I never expected to become so strong in rowing. We laughed and rowed loudly to overtake the cruise ships, which slowed down as they entered the harbor; this made the captains get angry, and they would honk repeatedly at us. Years later, when I was in the merchant navy traveling the vast ocean, I would see dolphins doing the same thing trying to compete with the speed of the ship.

For summer entertainment, we went to the open-air Rex cinema in town. There was also the Winter Palace Theatre, which operates until today. The movies I watched were John Wayne cowboy movies. All had Greek subtitles. I remember a black-and-white film called *Les Misérables*, which is a film adaptation from the famous novel by Victor Hugo. I realized how much strength it takes for one to forgive those who have harmed you, and of course it was God's power through that priest that represents God's grace, while God's law is against the sinner. Grace forgives, and it is grace that saved the soul of the play's main character, Jean Valjean. It was God who changed him. This story moves me to this day. However, the best films I liked to see on screen were the Christian ones, which were shown at Christmas and Easter and were about the life of Jesus and His words in the Sermon on the Mount. I could not understand then how He was so wise, good, and strong. We never had a Bible in our house, and I didn't know Jesus was the Son of God! About ten years later, He would enter my life and show me who He was, what He did on the cross to forgive me, and give me eternal life. He would also reveal to me His plan for my life according to His will.

We didn't have TV in Greece, so we listened and watched the latest news in the first five minutes before the movie. It was Greek and European news. For daily information, we only had the radio, which also broadcasted plays on weekend evenings. Everyone was crammed around the radio to listen to the broadcast, and it was the time when everyone was absolutely quiet.

On November of 1963, we heard on the radio that President Kennedy had been assassinated. Greece was very pro-American at the time, and the whole country experienced days of mourning for this loss. I remember my mother crying for weeks! Personally, our family benefited greatly from the food and clothing that the US government had sent for school children in our impoverished country.

I was there when they made this movie.

MY YEARS IN
HIGH SCHOOL

When I was in high school, the whole island was stirred up by the fact that a film company had chosen Rhodes to shoot the film *The Guns of Navarone* with Anthony Quinn, Gregory Peck, Stanley Baker, David Niven, Gia Scala, and Irene Papas. In 1961, it won seven Oscars. The city's two newspapers reported only on this event in the months they were filming there. They took extra soldiers from the Greek army and dressed them up as German soldiers. While in the field in front of our high school, they brought special painting teams to paint on all the trucks and tanks of the Greek army with the well-known German swastika.

Twenty years earlier, the Germans had come to the island as occupiers, but now these "Germans" were just actors. In the midst of all this turmoil, how could 1,200 boys and girls be kept in their classrooms along with 30–50 teachers? The daily newspaper informed us of where the filming would take place the next day. They used the beaches and castle of the island for many scenes.

Anthony Quinn fell so much in love with the island that he declared at one point: "I am not American but Greek!" He loved Greek food and dances. With a few thousand dollars, he bought a large coastal area, but because he did not develop it, it was given back to the city. To this day, they call it "Anthony Quinn's beach." During breaks and after school, we would run to where the movie was being shot. I was very impressed that while they were directing a scene from the play for days, they were filming it for just ten minutes! I was also impressed with Anthony Quinn. He wanted to have relationships with the people of the city, and you would often see him walking around the city center and chatting with the local merchants. Our principal was upset in those days because many children didn't come to school during the filming of the movie. There were few phones at the time, so parents couldn't tell them that their child was "sick." Thus, many children were simply absent from school.

The few hotels in the city were full of actors, technicians, and "German" Greek soldiers. I would suggest you check out this movie! I was there when Anthony Quinn grabbed a German soldier and threw him off the castle bridge. Before that happened, they had filmed the scene with the soldier lying down on the ground, as if he had landed there from the fall. Then they stacked several boxes and mattresses up to the bridge and filmed the time he fell down. Today, with the evolution of technology, everything is computerized and artificial, but back then, the scenes were real. While we were there watching, we were not allowed to talk or make the slightest noise.

Another great event I remember is when in 1961–62, the Cypriot victorious fighters of EOKA came to live on the island of Rhodes at the invitation of the mayor, Mr. Petrides. All over the island, we celebrated with joy and full of national pride, welcoming the heroes with their leader, Georgios Grivas (Digenis), who fought for the independence of Cyprus. I have never, in my life, seen such manifestations of national joy. These handsome young men found homes and jobs and brought their families to live with peace from their victory on the island of Rhodes.

Casting workshop

Welding and Machine Shop

The mayor of the city, Michael Petrides, a dentist by profession, was voted into office several times. One of the teachers we knew in Egypt, Dr. Paliouris—who was the principal of our Patriarchal School in Cairo—knew the mayor and my father. So he came to Rhodes and worked as a high school teacher at the Business Academy. With his help, my father found a job at a newly founded polytechnic school, where he would teach students who wanted a degree in technical engineering and could not afford to go to study in Athens. In the Dodecanese, there were many poor young people who could not go to study in Athens, so the Greek government established this school in Rhodes for those students who wanted to become engineers, radio communications engineers, and merchant marine engineers. Classes were held daily from 8:00 a.m. to 5:00 p.m. and were completely free. All students worked eight hours, six days a week, with their only pay being that of learning the trade.

The students, depending on their performance, were sent by the school to workplaces in the city for more technical training. They worked there for internships, earning a salary (although it was quite low). In the school, there was an electric motor department, a casting department (where aluminum and cast iron were melted and molded), a carpentry department, a machine shop (the largest in all the islands), a welding workshop, a boiler room, electric generators, etc. My father got a job as a technician in this place and was well paid, seventy-five drachmas a day (2.50 dollars), which was very good money at the time. At home we had no luxury items; we got a pair of shoes every year and had the necessary food. We didn't throw away our old shoes, but we took them to the cobbler, and he put on new soles so we could use them again. My mother worked as a seamstress in the city, and we were very happy. Joy returned to the family.

I was fifteen years old, as I stated before, when I went to this Polytech technical school and graduated at the age of nineteen. I got a degree in mechanical engineering for the Merchant Marine. My years at the school were very difficult because we worked very hard. We worked from eight to five in the various departments, and in the evening from six to ten, we attended theoretical classes. We attended classes from Monday to Saturday. On Sunday we had technical drawing classes from 8:00 a.m. until noon. Only on Sunday afternoon we had free time.

During the summer we had no theoretical classes, but we worked six days a week in the various departments, without pay. We spent six months in each class to train in it. I first went to the machine shop, where there were many lathes, milling machines, and other machinery, and we were learning how to use everything well. My father was the practical trainer in this workshop.

The second internship I went to was the welding workshop. We learned how to weld steel, brass, and even aluminum. All this was preparation for future work on a ship. Sometimes the school was contracted for paid work in the city for welding, casting, and electrical installations in buildings and hotels. And if the trainees had to work outside, they also received a salary. So they asked the school for technicians for building work, which included welding and electrical installations, because they were very good professionals. It was the time when hotels were built in Rhodes and contractors preferred the technicians of the schools because they gave them lower pay for the work.

The next department I worked in was a metal casting shop. We melted cast iron, brass, and aluminum. For three weeks we made the casts in sand on the ground with a special wood model, then followed with a week of a drying period with the cast on the ground. In the meantime, we were brought whole loads of old machines, manhole caps, cast-iron pipes, and we had to break them all into small pieces using sledgehammers. We also had competitions on who could hit them harder and longer so that they were small enough and ready to melt. We laid sand and cement in the bucket before pouring the molten metal. Within a day we had to melt the metal in a large oven with fifty-kilogram buckets fixed to long bars (held by four men) and pour the molten metal into molds. The temperature in the whole place was extremely high and smelled of sulfur. If the mold was not completely dry and had a trace of moisture, the molten metal would eject it, violently. When this happened, we had to drop the pouring bucket of molten metal and immediately run for cover. It was scary and dangerous to see the hot, molten metal exploding everywhere!

We manufactured manhole covers for the whole city of Rhodes, but also large brass valves for the water company. After the casting was complete, the items were transported to the machine shop, where they took their final form. I can still point out some items we cast that were placed around the city. They are still there in plain sight!

The next department I worked at was the electrical department. It was divided into two training grounds: one for electric motors and one for electrical installations in buildings. I was going to stay there for six months, but in the end, I stayed two years. Later, I made the blueprints myself, as well as installing the cables and inspecting the work. The chief electrician in this department was named Michalis. The electrical installation at the hotel-restaurant Rodini was completed by our school. The school sent us out into the city to make electrical installations, and I did the blueprints for them at the school and worked with them, installing them at Rodini. Upon completion of the work, the inspector of the city's electrical company would come and do the relevant inspection but rarely made changes because everything had been installed according to the city's plans.

Rodini Park—the oldest in Rhodes

In another laboratory department were the electric generators, which produce electricity using oil in the middle of the oceans. The whole point was for the trainees to be able to solve any problem they would encounter in the future on a ship.

Another department was carpentry. The school made windows and doors for the city, and we used machinery to complete the work. The carpentry specialist was an elderly man from Alexandria, Egypt. His specialty was to make casts for the casting department. He made them a little bigger so that when the hot metal was poured after it was cooled, they would shrink to the right size. He had a big nose and always joked that he couldn't drink ouzo in small glasses, so he drank it in large glasses, not tiny ones. But he didn't say this as a joke because every night he got drunk, drinking a lot of ouzo. Another good carpenter was the father of my good friend, Michael, whose name was Nikitas Hadjigeorgiou, and came from Aperi, Karpathos.

The instructor in the electric motor department was a Greek Italian named Negropontis. He had two sons aged sixteen and nineteen. Unfortunately, he sent his nineteen-year-old son to town for a 220-volt electrical installation and was electrocuted by the current, falling down dead. He never recovered from the loss of his son.

There was also a department at the school where we learned how to plate gold and silver onto various items that the city would give as gifts to tourists as they came off cruise ships. The entire educational system of the school and the perfect organization were due to the long-time brilliant mayor of Rhodes, Michael Petrides. He was a legend who will go down in history. He brought the best technicians and engineers from all over Greece to create and compete with other polytechnic and mechanical schools in Greece. He was the one who got my father a better job. How can we forget him?

Curiously, six months after my father was hired for this job, all the technicians went on strike for higher wages. I remember that my father came home one day very sad and told us that the mayor met him at school and reprimanded him, saying, "I tried to get you out of the window to get you a job, and now you want to walk out the door?" He meant that he had tried hard to find him a job and he had turned against him, siding with the strikers.

Rhodes was a poor city, and thanks to the efforts of this mayor, it is now one of the best and richest cities in Greece because he made it known throughout Europe as a tourist center.

I remember, the first lesson we did in the machine shop was cutting a steel shaft, ten centimeters in diameter, with a hacksaw in one day. The purpose was to learn how to cut metal straight, but also to get blisters on our tender hands. Then we compared the blisters with each other to see who had the biggest ones. If the slice or cut was straight, we got a good grade. Our instructor's name was Kostantaras, and he was from Piraeus. He was superintendent of the entire school. He bought a large estate in Rhodes and built a three bedroom U-shaped house. The entire backyard (one acre) was on the mountainside. Every day he sent four to five students to his house to level the mountainside so that he could plant. So we dug the soil uphill and threw it downhill. All day we fooled around, and just before he came home around four o'clock, we worked very hard for him to see us sweaty. His wife was a good cook, and we ate well.

Runaway cart

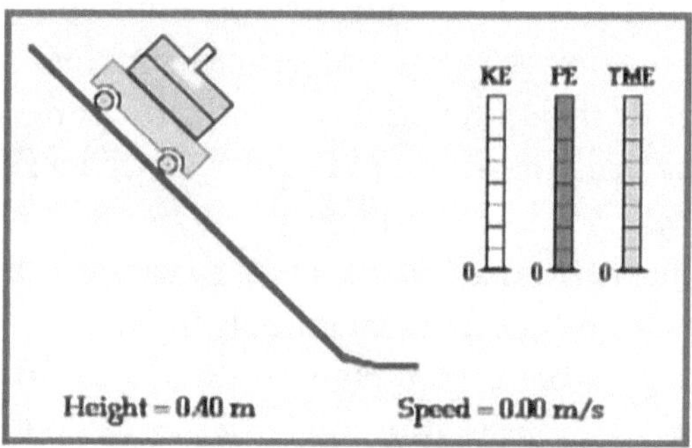

Mr. Kostantaras once wanted a fence with metal doors, and the fences he wanted would go around his house and his garden. He asked the school to buy metal for students to practice cutting and welding. We were constantly measuring and welding iron for him. After we finished welding, he asked us to make a cart to transport them to his estate. We made a cart two to three meters long with wood and metal and steel wheels of thirty centimeters in diameter with bearings in the center and with shafts. The front wheels rotated to steer the cart like a rudder. We loaded the metal parts onto the cart we had made and pushed it with our hands to his estate, about seven kilometers away from the school. The building of the school was on a hill, and his house was down on the beach. On this cart we built, one person sat in the front holding the rudder to steer the cart. As long as we were moving on flat ground, everything was fine. But when we started going downhill, the cart developed speed. We tried to keep it from going so fast, but we couldn't! The soles of our shoes were dragged on the asphalt to slow it down, but it was in vain. We made the cart to move, but not to stop! We forgot to put brakes on it! We violated street laws by running Warning signs and Stop signs and overtook buses and cars that honked at us repeatedly. It was a miracle that we didn't get killed running so fast, without hitting anyone or anything on the way. The second time we carried the same load, we took more precautions and made it so that it doesn't move as fast by putting a wooden brake system on it.

When I started attending the engineering school, I was just fifteen, and the other students were in their twenties. The few friends I hung out with were about my age or a little older. Three of my best friends were Manolis Papamichael, who lived in the village of Embona in Rhodes; Odeseas Papapanagiotis; and Michalis Hadjigeorgiou.

(Left) With my friend Manolis, who is the best
wine producer in the world, in my opinion
(Right) With my friend Odeseas, chief engineer, who
was present at my accident on the ship in 1966

We made the best jokes with my friend Manolis. He would cut vine branches, hang them on his head, and walk down the street, talking in a serious tone. We tried not to laugh and talked about various serious issues. We spoke loudly and impressed those around us.

Good, edible sea urchins

Quite often I would rent a bike to go to the east side of the island, four to five kilometers away, in a wild and rocky area, to swim and collect sea urchins with my knife. As I was alone, I hid my bike in the bushes, near the road, and then, passing by some farms, I would go down to the rocks and jump into the sea. I would dive to the bottom with a snorkel so that I could reach the bottom of the rocks, and with knife in hand, I would spot the good, tasty, large sea urchins. They are of different colors with small thorns on their backs. Black ones are poisonous, and I didn't pick them up. I would fill some bags with many and then go back home. But before I returned, I broke and ate five to ten of them right there on the rocky shore. Our neighbors begged me to give them a few because they were very delicious.

One Easter, I had a bad experience. I liked to light the makeshift firecrackers and make them explode. My friend, George Charitos, showed me how to make triangular and square firecrackers. I improved the technique, so we made huge firecrackers. The usual square firecrackers had a side of three to four centimeters, and I made them with a side of seven centimeters. We found some tar paper from old construction sites and bought smokeless gunpowder in a one-liter can from hunting shops for about thirty drachmas. We wrapped a few tablespoons of gunpowder in the paper until it became four centimeters thick. We carefully made a hole in the center to get to the black powder, and very carefully, we wedged into the hole some matches with sulfur heads. Now I know how dangerous it was, but then, I thought it was just a fun game. I rubbed the matches with a sharp movement on the side of the matchbox to light up and at the same time threw the firecracker away. A big explosion followed, scattering small pieces of tar everywhere, and that amused me very much.

But I'll tell you what happened to the last firecracker I made. I thought the flame from the matches hadn't reached all the way down to the center, so I turned it around to see, and that's when it exploded in my hand! I was showing off in front of my father. I pretended that everything was fine, but I thought I lost my right arm! I ran to the corner of the yard and saw my hand. It was black from the blood that burst from the blood vessels. It was numb, and I couldn't feel anything. I ran to a neighbor's house and put it under cold water. My hand was swollen and twice it's normal size, and I couldn't move my fingers. I could feel the outside of my hand but not the inside. For three weeks I couldn't use it. I had to tell everyone who asked me what had happened.

In Rhodes, it was very common to see children without arms or legs. This is because, when World War II ended and before the construction of hotels along the beaches, there were fortifications of guns and machine guns, and in the sand, there were buried shell casings of brass projectiles. Sometimes you could even find intact projectiles. Many children tried to remove the head of the projectile from the shell, causing it to explode. Thus, they lost arms and legs. There are still some fortifications all over the island, but now they are empty. At that time many poor people used these fortifications as houses. On the eastern side of the island, there was a large fortification where a gypsy family lived. After nearly losing my hand and ruining my life and future, I never used firecrackers again. I do not recommend anyone to try it because it is too dangerous.

A SIGNIFICANT EVENT ON CHRISTMAS DAY

I remember when I was seventeen years old, in the early morning of Christmas Day, we went to church around 4:30 a.m. for the Christmas liturgy with my friend Dimitris Kalafatis. We didn't go inside, but we stayed outside the church and chatted, laughing at various jokes, while the service went on. Our parents were very proud that we went to mass so early. Suddenly we saw a big light shining on the eastern horizon! It was very bright and formed a cross in the night sky. We were left staring at it in shock for a few seconds, and then I told Dimitris to go inside and bring the priest to see it. But he did not want to interrupt the priest in the middle of the service and did not go in. So, after a while, the light disappeared. I was afraid, but I was sure that we saw it and that God wanted to show us this event so we would believe that Christmas is true. I began to not doubt the existence of God.

After graduating from the engineering school, I had to complete various government documents and join the Greek army to fulfill my military obligations. I reported to the Naval Recruitment Center in the Peloponnese (Southern Greece). When they found out that I was a refugee from the war in Egypt, they told me that they could exempt me from military service if I paid a small amount of money. The reasoning behind it was that the Greek government could not help refugees at the time of the war, so it allowed the sons of the families to be exempted from military service and join the workforce directly to help their families. I didn't serve in the navy because I was the son of a refugee from Egypt. They gave me official documents that I was free now to travel around the world "as an untrained soldier."

Two months after the end of my studies at the Polytech Marine Engineering School, a friend of the family, who was a second engineer on the ship *PARNON*, asked me to enlist as an apprentice engineer on his ship. It was a 15,000-ton mineral cargo ship. So, in September 1965, I joined the ship as an apprentice engineer from the port of Pylos, in the Peloponnese.

My seaman's (marine) passport

PART 2

In the autumn of 1965, as I have already mentioned, I joined the ship *PARNON* as an apprentice engineer. Our first trip was to go from the port of Pylos in the Peloponnese, Greece, to Aberdeen in Scotland and load iron minerals for Japan. This was the first experience I had on a merchant ship.

The *PARNON* was a Greek ship built in England in 1935.
(The photo is a similar ship.)

The ship *PARNON* painted in a shell

Street vendors painted our ship on a shell, and we bought it as a souvenir. You can see in the photos the shape of the ship, as well as the size of this beautiful shell, which I bought from the city of Cebu, Philippines.

The ship had a Bulmeister diesel engine, the cylinders of which had openings in the lower part of the cylinder, and every time the piston went up and down, you could see the low part of the piston while sparks, fumes, and dirty lubricants flew around. The engine room was always full of smoke, which made breathing very difficult. You couldn't see as you go down the stairs to the lower floors because of the smoke. There were fans that brought fresh air into the engine room; however, it could not reach all areas. We had to repair everything that broke ourselves on this old and broken ship. I felt nauseous for weeks and couldn't eat anything since I vomited day and night; as a result, I lost a lot of weight. It was a horrible experience, and to this day I have nightmares, that I am down in the engine room inside the dark, smoky, and dirty ship. In this situation, I worked the four-to-eight shift in the morning and evening and had four to six hours overtime a day, seven days a week with no weekend off.

The chief engineer—I am not mentioning his name—was very intelligent but tough, demanding more and more work, without paying all the overtime, when it came time to pay. The second engineer was his brother-in-law and was just as tough. There were only a few crew members in the engine room: a janitor, three engineers, three apprentice engineers (one was me), a second engineer, and the first engineer—that is, a small crew for a huge ship, to save money. The food was awful with old frozen meat, while the quantity was not enough for a crew that worked so hard. The metal rooms we slept in were unbearably hot, next to the engine room, with two or three people in the same room. Horrible conditions! At the time, I didn't know that God was watching over me and teaching me to stay the course in adverse circumstances.

One of the worst jobs on the ship, which I will never forget, was when I was assigned to clean the dirty oil of the ship's double bottom, as well as the filters that were under the engine base. The place was dark and slippery, while the walls and floor were coated with a thick layer of used oil. I had to crawl through a room with a ceiling 1/2 meter high and a floor 30 meters long, covered with 10 centimeters of gel oil, to reach the filters and clean them. I only had a wrench in my pocket and a flashlight in my hand to see. It was very scary as I heard and felt beneath me the vibration of the ocean in the belly of the ship!

Another dangerous job I was assigned to do was fill a bucket with sulfuric acid and carry it down the steep stairs to the boilers and engine coolers to be cleaned. Once, I remember, acid splashed my leather shoes, punctured my leather and socks, and burned my foot to the bone! I had to rinse it immediately with water to dilute the acid, but by the time I got to where the water was, the damage was done. I had a wound there for over two months. I wrapped my shoes in strips of fabric and a leather belt to protect them from more damage and allow me to carry on my workload as usual.

I had to do my best to get a good report from the chief engineer when I left this ship to go to another. I had to endure hardships, which are my nightmares even today! So I worked very hard. I was very strong, and I did the best I could in these terrible conditions. Hard work has been a challenge for me and has helped me to endure and become stronger.

The young janitor we had on board, after six months of working under these inhumane conditions, fell ill with tuberculosis and, at the first port, was diagnosed and sent back to Greece for treatment. His position was never filled, so the apprentices (I was one of them) had to do his job as well. Many times, small fires broke out in the engine room. That's why every ten meters we had fire extinguishers. On the deck of the ship, there were five holds, holding a total of 15,000 tons of cargo.

COMMUNIST RUSSIA, AS IT WAS THEN

The ship *Meandros*

The ship *PENTAS*

When we went to Vladivostok, Russia, we saw giant shirtless workers while it was snowing, loading hundreds of kilos of bags of coal on their shoulders and climbing up a wooden ramp to the ship, to throw it in the hold. This kind of loading went on for over a week. There was snow on the ground, and it snowed constantly.

We wanted to go out a few times, to get a bottled drink and see the city, but it was very difficult to do that. To get off the ship, we had to be fingerprinted and signed various documents and government forms. It was a great inconvenience to do so. Inside a caged room were Russian soldiers who gave us a pass only to cross the dock, while at another gate they had to fingerprint us again. After that, we were accompanied by a soldier who showed us around the city on an open-top bus in freezing weather! We saw huge buildings of fifteen to twenty floors without windows. On the walls were painted giant pictures of Lenin, Stalin, and workers with sickles harvesting wheat. Depressing areas. Then we stopped at a place where we could get out and stood in a line to buy a bottled drink. We had to stand there to drink it, and then they took us back to the boat in the open-top bus. All the time, the driver of our group, who was Russian, speaking fluent Greek, was telling us how wonderful the country of Russia and the system of communism was. We didn't dare say anything and just looked each other in the eye with a small smile. Sailors who travel around the world see the difference firsthand. From there we went to Japan to unload the cargo in Muroran, Hokkaido.

Empty ship going to the Philippines, islands of coconuts

After that, by empty ship we traveled south, to the Philippine Islands, to load coconuts for Los Angeles, California. Along the way, we were suddenly hit by a very strong storm. The empty ship was going up and down so badly, the wind was so strong, and the ship was shaking from side to side, over a day and night. In the middle of the night, we heard a very loud noise from the back of the ship rolling and being crushed on the sides of the ship. Some sailors sent by the captain opened the covers of the last empty hold of the ship, and to their surprise, the spare shaft of the propeller was loose and flowed freely in the hold and was hitting the sides of the ship. The spare propeller shaft had been fixed with clamps that had rusted and loosened with the tremor of the force of the waves hitting the sides of the ship in the storm. From those blows to the wall of the ship, seawater penetrated through the openings! I believe this was also because the wall plates of the ship were not welded but were connected by rusty rivets. We didn't know where we were going because the boat was being dragged back and forth in the rough sea, traveling against the storm. This went on for a long time, and the condition of the ship was getting worse and worse. Almost half of the ship's hold was full of water. We feared for our lives and thought that at any moment, the ship would sink and no one would know about it or be able to save us. We activated all the emergency pumps in the engine room to pump the water out of the hold and transfer it to the first hold for balance. All the engineers and all the assistants were down in the engine room, starting all the generators to generate electricity for all the balance pumps, electric pumps, and steam pumps and to draw the water from hold 5. We did everything, but it seemed that the results were very small.

The captain eventually turned the ship back to Japan. The radio operator constantly called the Japanese tugs for help. We were very close to Osaka, Japan. These storms occur very often in autumn in southern Japan and are the worst. Then, quite unexpectedly, all the moving of the ship stopped. (At times like these, when people are close to seeing their Creator, they think very seriously about God; so I, too, prayed for God to save us.) Everything became calm except for the wind. We were in Osaka Bay. It was quiet, the ship was stabilized, and we all ran from the engine room onto the deck to see what had happened. Two large tugboats were waiting for us and brought us safely to a dock for a week of repairs. They put the spare propeller shaft in its place, fixing it with new straps to stabilize it, replaced the rivets loosened on the sides of the ship, painted its exterior, and within a week, had repaired it entirely. Amazing Japanese workers! All of us on board thanked God for saving our lives!

Our trip continues to the Philippines

In the fall of 1965, we went to the ports of Cebu, Masbate, Tagbilaran, and Zamboanga in the Philippines.

A funny incident happened on this trip. Makis, a young sailor of about twenty-five years old, had a portable turntable with batteries and played Beatles songs day and night. He worked, painted, and had the turntable always by his side to play. Over time I began to like it. The song "A Hard Day's Night" was played over and over and over again. I had been taking English lessons in Greece for over seven years, but I could not speak a word. I understood the English I was reading, but to speak it and be understood by others was almost impossible. I remember a song from the first Beatles album called "I'm a Loser." Makis asked me if I knew what they were singing, and when I told him no, he started explaining to me about the song. He told me it was the story of an Indian boy who lost his horse named Appaloosa because an evil cowboy shot and killed it. The little boy did not know what had happened to it and went wandering in the mountains calling for his horse to return to him: "Appaloosa, Appaloosa." It was such a sad story, it brought tears to my eyes! I was very angry with the ruthless cowboy for doing something so cruel! However, years later, I learned that the song was not about any lost horse, but the singer was simply saying that he was "a loser" ("I am a loser," that is, a failure in life). Ah, that Makis!

After the great adventure in the ocean near Osaka, we finally arrived in the Philippines. I recall that Cebu City was very impressive with its Catholic churches, universities, and good and kind people. But when we went to Zamboanga City, another port in the Philippines, we were warned not to go out wearing watches or jewelry or having lots of money on us. We were to walk in groups and return to the ship before midnight. There was also an American there in town who had a circus with animals and a round cage (the Wooden Barrel). Inside he showed off, driving his motorcycle quickly around, with his Filipino wife holding onto him. We paid fifty cents for the ticket, to see this show.

Death Lap

The next morning, we learned about the horrific event that happened to the first engineer of another Greek ship, which was in port next to our ship. The engineer had gone out late, and while returning alone, someone killed him just to steal his watch! On the island of Zamboanga, people's faces were very wild. I learned that in Cebu City, citizens are Catholics, but in Zamboanga, they are Muslims.

From the Philippines we loaded 15,000 tons of coconuts, to transport them to Los Angeles, California, USA, for cosmetics companies. The coconuts were carried in baskets on the shoulders by men and women workers from various villages, who carried them up the ramp and threw them into the ship's holds. We were warned that after a few weeks, billions of small flies would hatch from the coconuts, and so it happened! The holds were hot because of the rotten coconuts. Traveling across the ocean, flies flew around the ship, entering through the windows into our rooms, the kitchen, and even over our food! We closed the holds to keep them inside, but that didn't help much.

We crossed the Pacific Ocean and arrived in the famous city of Los Angeles around Christmas time. It was the first time I saw California, and I loved it very much! Entering the port, we were very impressed by the thousands of Christmas lights on the buoys and the Vincent Thomas bridge all lit up in lights. How beautiful the city was with all those illuminated Christmas trees everywhere!

WAS THIS THE AMERICA I WAS HEARING ABOUT?

We entered the port after midnight on December 24, 1965. After the ship docked, around two in the morning, two men climbed up the ramp to our loaded ship to give us temporary passes to go ashore. We saw a third middle-aged man standing on the dock, who most people knew, and they called him Mr. Marangakis, which in Greek means "little carpenter." I asked who he was, and they told me he was a religious man trying to talk to us about God. The immigration office gave passes to all of us, even though there was a possibility that we would abandon the ship and stay in the USA. An American officer wished us a "Merry Christmas," and I wondered what that meant. Many joked about the way he pronounced the phrase and said it sounded like "many days in crisis."

Then the third man—about sixty years old, burly, with a short, small mustache—walked toward us and asked if we were all Greeks. He wished us a "Merry Christmas" in Greek, and then, opening his bag, began handing out New Testaments to the entire crew. He stopped a moment, and I asked him, "What's your name?"

He said, "Manolis Marangakis. What's your name?"

I replied, "My name is Peter."

"What a beautiful name!" he said to me and continued. "Peter, take this Bible, read it, and do not sin, my child! I want you to know, Peter, God loves you!"

Mr. Marangakis while cooking in church, with his wife, Dolly

The little blue book he gave me

I was shocked and confused. What reasonable person would leave his family at 2:00 a.m. and come on a ship to distribute New Testaments on Christmas Day? Let alone that he had to wait an hour or two in the cold until he boarded the ship, wearing only an ordinary suit with a coat. After he left, we all talked about him. He didn't look crazy, and maybe he was paid well by someone to do that; we didn't know his motives. I never heard that God loves me or that Jesus loves me. I was Greek Orthodox and went to church all my life, but *I never heard those words*! No one ever gave me a Bible, nor did I have hope that God loves me!

I still believe that I am Greek Orthodox, but now I live the true meaning of the phrase "true pilgrim, who truly worships God."

Before, I didn't know God. I worshipped my ideas and what I learned from relatives, friends, and school about God. Today I worship the true God, having accepted and believed the true gospel, which is that Jesus died for our sins and rose again for our justification.

Mr. Marangakis was a kind man and gave me a Bible for free. I believe God had begun to work in my heart. Before leaving, he told us that after our breakfast on the ship, he would come back to take us to church. Then we went to bed. I was so excited! I was looking out of the porthole of my room, seeing the illuminated harbor and thinking of this man, Mr. Marangakis. I thought he could be sent by God. He didn't say anything bad to me, saying that God loves me. I had never heard anything like this! In the morning, after checking the generators in the engine room of the ship, I was free for the whole day, and then Mr. Marangakis came and took us to church for the Christmas service.

This church was different, clean and simple, without icons and gold decorations on the walls. Another difference was that the priest did not have a beard and spoke from the Bible in today's language. He was passing on to us what he was reading to us, and I began to understand some of God's things for the first time in my life. I remember him telling us that the reason Jesus came to earth was to pay the penalty for our sins on the cross and that three days later, He rose from the grave. The priest said that whoever truly believes in Jesus, God will enable him to become a new man. After the message, Christians welcomed us with love and respect and were very friendly and took us to the dining room for a Christmas dinner. They didn't have ashtrays on the tables because no one smoked, and they were kind to each other and especially to the elderly. They were true Christians who had love for one another, for God, and for strangers. We never felt like strangers in this church. I have been to many ports, where people came with free buses to take us to the bars of the city, and then we had to find our way back to the ship by taxi. However, Mr. Marangakis came and took us back to our ship after the dinner. He told us that he would return the following Sunday to take us back to the evening church meeting. He was driving a Chevy station wagon that could fit seven to eight sailors. It was the first time

I began to seriously think that "God loves me" and that God could be true and that He cared about me! Mr. Marangakis's words were followed by his act of love. How can I deny his words?

Mr. Marangakis's car

Soon we would leave the port of Long Beach with the best impressions of America—beautiful California, Mr. Marangakis, the church, and Pastor Deligiannis, who spoke passionately from the Bible. We stayed in the Port of Los Angeles for one week.

DOES GOD ANSWER
THE PRAYERS OF
SOMEONE WHO DOES
NOT YET KNOW HIM?

I worked very hard in the engine room as an apprentice. The engine room had four floors, and after the first floor you could not see because of the smoke coming out of the engines. I have never smoked in my life, and yet I breathed exhaust fumes in the engine room at least twelve hours a day. The food on board was not of the best quality, although the cook did his best with what he had. For example, on Saturday we were served lamb shank with pasta. Delicious!

Even though I worked more than 100–150 hours overtime a month, the first engineer wouldn't pay me for overtime because he said he would have a problem with the office. I was making about £30 a month. But I was patient. I was a career man, and I had to work hard to get a good report from the chief engineer, who threatened me that if I demanded my overtime, he would write on my resume that I was a "communist," which was the worst thing for someone in those days. Of course I wasn't a communist, but he used it as a threat. I had the worst and then the best experiences on this ship. The best of all was when a stranger in the Port of Los Angeles said to me, "Peter, God loves you!" and gave me hope for the future and great joy.

At the Port of Los Angeles, we unloaded thousands of tons of coconuts. We had stayed in port until New Year's Day, and now with our ship empty, we were preparing to go north to pick up timber from the states of Portland, Oregon, and Washington for Liverpool, England.

SIGN FROM GOD?

I was in the engine room at about 3:00–4:00 p.m. on New Year's Day 1966, and we were getting ready to leave the Port of Los Angeles. I was next to the first engineer as an apprentice, to learn the navigation maneuvers of the ship's entry and exit from the port. We turned on all the compressors to start the engine. The communication of the captain on the navigation bridge with the chief engineer in the engine room is done using a telegraph, with navigation orders, "FORWARD—STOP—REVERSE."

The captain and pilot instructed the chief engineer via telegraph to go slowly forward. But the ship was going backward, and the first engineer, who had full control of the engine, gave more throttle and the ship went further back. Then the captain, through the telegraph, gave the order to move forward, but the chief engineer did the reverse. Instead of going forward, the ship went backward! For a moment I saw what was happening and said to the first engineer, "We are going backwards!" But he was very nervous and cursed at me, as if I knew nothing, and went further backward. The captain's order was now to go full speed forward, but the ship was in reverse full speed!

A week earlier (I must mention it now), when I had gone to church with Mr. Marangakis, I saw very good people singing wonderful hymns and praying. This new church was different, and I loved it. I wondered if there was a God I didn't know about. I prayed to God and asked Him to allow me to stay here for another month to go to this new church. But now, I was on the ship leaving the Port of Los Angeles, and I thought my prayer would go unanswered.

The ship was going backward, while the captain's order was "full speed ahead." We were going completely in reverse, while for a minute or two, signals were constantly coming from the bridge to the engine room, "Full speed ahead." The ship's propeller started hitting the concrete dock and shaking the whole ship! The first engineer nervously turned off all the engines and ran upstairs to see what the problem was, while the captain and the American pilot ran to see what was happening down in the engine room. Thus, the captain and the chief engineer reported that the engine was unresponsive and the ship was going in the opposite direction, which is technically impossible. The first engineer was very nervous and confused and accidentally put the ship in reverse, thinking it was going forward; as a result, the huge 90 rpm propeller, seven meters in diameter, hit the concrete dock. We were all left staring dumbfounded. I knew the truth. The first engineer gave a false report of what had happened so that the insurance company could pay for the damage. (For this reason, I do not mention names.) Then I remembered my prayer to God. Maybe it was from God?

The ship was then placed in a special dry dock for repairs. It was a month before we received a new propeller and rudder from England, and then we waited for the repairs to be finished. They turned off all the engines, which meant we wouldn't have any work on board! Our ship was at Bethlehem Steel Shipyard on Terminal Island. (Nine years later, I would be working as an engineer at *this* shipyard with my legal green card; however, there is another story to tell first.)

Deep in my heart, I wondered if this was from God. Until the repairs were finished, I could go to church again with Brother

Marangakis. I called him and told him what had happened on the dock. He lived in San Gabriel on Emerson Street with his wife, Dolly, and two sons, Chris and Timothy. Every Wednesday and Sunday he would come, and we would go to church. We were very, very happy. He would take us to his house for dinner, stew and chicken with spaghetti. Often, he would come and take us to his restaurant, Big Bun on Garvey Avenue. We didn't work on the ship in those days and just sat watching the repairs. The insurance company paid for all damages. These were wonderful days.

A month later, after the repairs were made, we left port and went north to Portland, Coos Bay, and Tacoma, Washington, receiving 15,000 tons of timber, and traveled down the coast through the Panama Canal up the Atlantic coast to Liverpool, England, where we unloaded the timber. This load of wood that was three meters higher than the ship's deck created a balance problem, and the ship traveled at an angle of ten to fifteen degrees either left or right because the center of gravity was higher than normal.

We had been on board for over a year, and if we came to a port in Europe, we could get a free return to Greece at the shipowner's expense. So now was the opportunity to get off the ship and return to Greece. I was an apprentice and needed another six months of service on a ship to take the exam and get promoted to third engineer. I wanted so badly to leave this ship. I was trying to be calm and patient. On the ship I didn't spend money, but when we went to ports in Africa, Japan, and the Philippines, I bought a lot of things for my sisters. In America, I bought Cannon towels and sheets for all my sisters as dowry, which were very famous and expensive in Greece.

On our way to Liverpool, the captain and chief engineer wanted to ask me about something and invited me to the captain's office next to the bridge. The first engineer didn't like me and always gave me more work, without declaring to the company's headquarters the overtime I was doing. He was never satisfied with my work; the working conditions were unacceptable and perhaps illegal. He told me to go visit my family in Greece, and when I came back on the same ship, he would give me a promotion to the position of third engineer without taking an exam or getting any diploma. He had the ability to do that. I asked him if he liked my work on the ship. He said to me, "There is no one else who could do the job that you did, Peter." (I wish he had told me this earlier.) Continuing, the first engineer told me that "for me the bell was ringing" and that I was the best apprentice he ever had. He wanted to say my luck had changed!

Now he needed workers to do the work on this ship, and there weren't many who could or wanted to do it. The ship's reputation was very bad, and no one wanted to be hired on a ship that abused workers so badly. Of the thirty-five-or-so crew members, about thirty abandoned the ship at the first opportunity due to poor conditions and the harsh attitude of the employers. When the entire crew leaves a ship and does not return, it's a bad sign. When I left the ship, I said I'd try to come back, but I knew I would not.

The first engineer finally gave me a good report, I believe, to make me want to return to the ship, but this wasn't going to happen! It was an old and rusty ship, the food was awful, we had no clean water to drink, and we made our own drinking water from seawater using the boiler-evaporator! The conditions in the engine room were horrible, with all that stuffy smoke, and on top of that, they didn't even pay me overtime. Until today, I still have nightmares of being on that old ship and having to go down to the dark double bottom floor of the ship to clean the thick oil and water. I remained polite and kind to the captain and the first engineer, but I knew in my heart that I would not accept their offer. To this day, I'm not sure if the chief engineer's last-minute kindness was because he wanted me back on board or for me not to tell anyone in the company that the ship crashed in Long Beach by his mistake.

So, arriving in Liverpool, the company prepared my seaman's passport so that I could return to Greece at the company's expense and from Dover, England; along with the rest of the crew, we took a ferry to Calais, France. I had a suitcase full of gifts for my sisters and a second suitcase with my clothes. From France we took a train straight to Greece, and it took three days to get there. We passed through France, Germany, Yugoslavia, then we entered the small town of Idomeni in northern Greece, then on to Athens by train and then by boat to the island of Rhodes.

I finally got home and stayed there for about a month. I shared my experiences with my family and gave them the gifts I had bought from different countries. I still needed a few months of service on a ship before I could take the exam for a third engineering position, so I would have to enroll on another ship for the required experience. I had begun to believe that God answers prayers, so I prayed that He would help me find a better ship to continue my career as an apprentice engineer.

In Rhodes I met my friend Odeseas Papapanagiotis again. We agreed to go on the same boat together this time. So we went to Piraeus and looked to see which ships were available. With God's help, we found a shipping company, PENTAS. It was given this name by its five founders (Peratikos, Nomikos, Andreadis, Xylas, Pateras). In the office, everyone had friendly and sweet faces. They said they had a brand-new ship. One of the owners asked us if we wanted to work on their ship, and when we answered in the affirmative, he came and hugged us. The ship, weighing 45,000 tons, was built at Japan's Mitsubishi shipyard and was coming from Japan to the Netherlands for a new crew. It was three times larger than the previous ship I had worked on, so in just a few months, I found myself, again, as an apprentice, but on a new ship this time with my friend Odeseas.

The ship—*Pentas*

THE NEW SHIP—A VERY GOOD CHOICE

On board the ship *PENTAS* were some Japanese technicians who had tested out the ship all the way from Japan to the Netherlands. The ship's owners had given us money to go either by plane or train to the Netherlands. Eventually we went by train. They gave us a month's salary in advance so that we could return to Rhodes from Athens and say goodbye to our relatives before traveling.

We were a new crew of forty-five to fifty people who traveled from Athens to the Netherlands. We first stayed in a hotel in Rotterdam and then took a taxi to the dock. As we approached, we saw a huge ship! It was freshly painted, and everything about it was new. We went down to the control room of the ship and saw that everything was electronic. The control room area was a closed, air-conditioned room, and smoke-free. They had hired janitors, oilers, etc. for the ship, and we didn't have to do any other work, just work and control the engine. The food was amazing. What a wonderful ship! Both crew and officers were amazingly happy people.

We stayed a week with the Japanese workers on the ship before they left, but the Japanese chief engineer stayed on for one year. There were manuals and instruction books in Japanese and English for each part of the ship. The Japanese chief engineer had many books about the operation of the ship so that he knew exactly how to repair everything and trained us in the use of these books, because as Greeks we tend to correct things without following instructions. In the air-conditioned area of the engine room were pressure and temperature gauges. The captain of the ship was from Athens and had brought his son as an apprentice captain.

I was twenty-one years old. The ship, freshly painted as it was, did not need much maintenance. The captain's son was a very happy young man, and we quickly became friends. He wanted to be a writer of detective stories (Young Fleming's new James Bond). He didn't write very well though because he read me his stories and I didn't like his writing style, not that mine is better!

The ship traveled from Canada to Amsterdam and Rotterdam, transporting minerals to factories in Germany via small riverboats. We had a contract with Africa, Nigeria, and the Ivory Coast to load minerals for German factories. We also took minerals from the town of Luleå in Sweden and transported them to Germany. Many fell ill on this journey with the abrupt change in weather conditions because, from the hot summer in Africa, we found ourselves in the bitter cold of Sweden in the space of ten days.

Through the great canals of Amsterdam, narrow boats came to our ship and loaded minerals. These long narrow boats usually belonged to families who used them as their residence. They lived at one end of the boat, which had a kitchen and bedroom, with their father as captain and their wife and children as assistants. They even had dogs and flowerpots. They were small narrow boats but very beautiful and convenient. They carried their cargo deep into Germany, via the rivers. From Amsterdam, we sailed across the Atlantic and arrived at the port of Montreal, Canada. We went to Quebec to load mineral for Amsterdam. The journey took about fourteen days crossing the Atlantic. On August 6, 1966, I had a serious accident in the engine room, resulting in a deep cut in my left arm, *but God intervened again, saving my life.*

HOW IT ALL STARTED

Our ship was traveling from Amsterdam to Quebec, Canada, to Sept-Îles (Seven Islands port), to load iron mineral weighing forty-five thousand tons. It had already made two to three trips from Quebec to Amsterdam, loaded with minerals, and then returned empty to Quebec, to load a few more tons.

In Montreal, the ladder from which we descend from the ship to the port is adjustable so that it reaches the dock. It moves down and up to adapt to the height of the ship as it is loaded with minerals. We loaded the seven holds of the ship very quickly, using a conveyor belt, and within five to ten hours, all the holds were full. It should be noted that the ship is sinking in the water as tons of minerals are loaded into the holds. Unfortunately, the head of the sailors forgot to pull the pin that allows the ladder to go up and down the hinge as the ship sinks with increasing cargo. So the whole ladder bent in the shape of an L. They tried to remove the pin but were unsuccessful, so the captain said to leave it for the time being and they would repair it later at sea. His priority was to get the cargo quickly to the next port across the Atlantic Ocean.

As the ship moved away from the dock, the ladder, which was now very bent, jumped down from the dock, shaking the entire ship. It was now broken and useless and needed repair, but there was no time for it, so we left Montreal and went across the Atlantic, to the Netherlands, to unload the cargo. However, when we arrived in Amsterdam, the ship had to dock on the opposite side so we could deal with repairing the broken staircase.

On the way back to Quebec going across the ocean again, we were able to dismantle the ladder and fix the thirty-to-forty steps quite easily, but the steel square plate 2 × 2 meters wide and 4 centimeters thick at the top of the staircase was the hard part of the job, where the hinge was. We had to remove it, cut it into two pieces to bend it straight, and weld it again so that it was flat again. This work would be done down in the ship's machine shop by the second engineer and apprentice (me).

It was around August 6, 1966, as I said before. Together with the second engineer, we cut the steel plate with an oxygen torch into two pieces, using a crane, which held it up, because it was very heavy. The cutting was almost finished, but some welding spots still held the two pieces of steel plate together. We picked it up again, and the second engineer told me to hold the top piece while he hit the bottom with a hammer to break it apart. I was standing on a bench while the crane held the plate high in the air. The second engineer continued to hit the bottom piece repeatedly and forcefully while I held the upper part. I was feeling very uncomfortable about the technique. Eventually, the two pieces broke apart with their very sharp edges exposed. And then it happened!

The bottom piece, as it came off, fell and hit my arm and knee! Suddenly I saw blood everywhere! I was still standing on the bench while the second engineer was on the ground with the other piece of plate, and I asked him what had happened. He had no idea. I told him someone was bleeding, and because I didn't feel anything, I told him it must have been him. But then I turned around and saw my left arm open from the middle of the arm to the wrist. The nerves and veins could be seen down to the bone! The veins pulsated blood into the air. I realized to my horror that it was me who was bleeding! I sat down on the bench, got dizzy, and passed out right there. My hand was like a sandwich that, if you opened it, you could see everything inside. It was full of blood! They picked me up and took me to the area for the wounded or sick, near the captain's room. There was no doctor on board, no medicines, no other medical supplies, except aspirin and bandages.

Meanwhile, while all this was happening, our ship was passing through a terrible storm in the middle of the Atlantic, heading for Montreal, Canada. The ship was empty and very light, so it could move faster, but it shook in the storm. They tied my hand with a sheet very tightly to stop the bleeding. I was dizzy and started losing my sight and hearing due to blood loss, feeling overwhelmed. Every voice reached my ears like a muffled sound.

The second engineer blamed me for holding the plate, trying to justify the accident. The captain and the chief engineer went inside to see what they could do. I tried to speak, but I couldn't communicate because I was almost unconscious. My mouth was dry, and I didn't feel anything. I could hear them talking, but it was hard to understand what they were saying. But I remember the captain saying that maybe I would lose my arm because the cut was long and deep. He then told the engineer to increase the speed, to get to Montreal faster. Meanwhile, an English passenger ship full of doctors, medical supplies, etc. was crossing the Atlantic toward Europe. They radioed about my accident, and both ships stopped in the middle of the Atlantic during the storm to see if they could let down a small lifeboat to carry me across to the other ship. But the storm did not calm down, and it was very dangerous to do so. So, after eight to ten hours of waiting, hoping in vain that the storm would calm down, the two ships decided to abandon the attempt and continue their opposite destinations. I learned all these details after a month, when I returned to the ship healthy.

GUARDIAN ANGELS

Are not all angels ministering spirits sent to serve those who will inherit salvation? (Hebrews 1:14 NIV)

Meanwhile, I was a mess physically, struggling between life and death. I heard muffled sounds, felt no pain, and did not eat or drink anything. The second captain came and loosened the tourniquet, and then the blood flowed again, soaking the towel. My whole left arm was covered in dry blood. I couldn't move it. I was so sad and wondering if I would lose my arm or die! How would my mother feel?

At some point I heard a male voice in my right ear! His voice was very clear, slow and sweet, and with compassion, he said to me again and again in fluent Greek: "Peter, do not be afraid. You will not die. Something great is going to happen to you!" When I heard it, I felt like I was smiling inside. I reached out my right hand to touch the person who was talking to me, but there was no one there. I heard this voice many times during my seven-day trip to Montreal. They told me later that people were trying to feed me some soup, but I didn't remember anything.

When we arrived near the port, a speedboat came and I was lowered by crane to the hospital boat on a stretcher and I remember hearing a helicopter above me. All this movement and action woke me up, and I regained consciousness. Then I realized that I was very seriously ill. My arm was swollen and smelled very bad. I had a high fever and was shivering and couldn't speak. As soon as we reached land, I was immediately taken to the hospital by ambulance. The voice I heard on the ship stopped when I reached land, but it had given me confidence that I would not die and that something great was about to happen to me.

They took me to the Hospital Sept-Îles, which was next door to a university where medical students were studying. The nurses wore big hats and spoke French. Because I had learned a little French when I was in Egypt, I was able to communicate somewhat with the doctors and nurses. Then a doctor tried to see the wound, opening some of the bandages. I was screaming in pain while my heart beat so hard I thought it was going to come out of my chest! Indeed, I had never felt such pain in my life!

The doctor told me not to worry and stopped trying to open the wound. They gave me intravenous fluids and maybe even blood. Then they put my whole arm in a container with solution and let it soak for a few hours. Then the doctor let *me* remove the bandages as slowly as I could. The pain began to stop because they were giving me morphine. The pain was no longer felt, and I slowly removed the bandages. As soon as they were removed, they took me straight to the operating room. I woke up after the first operation, and they asked me how I felt. They asked me if I could move my fingers and feel anything. Thank God, I could! They said another operation would be performed in a week to complete the operation and heal the wound. After my operation, our ship loaded 45,000 tons of mineral and left for Amsterdam without me. They returned after a month, in September 1966.

The nurses who were nuns came every day to treat my wounds and pray for me, while a Catholic priest came and talked to me about the Lord. He was tall with gray hair. He told me that God loves me and that he would pray for me every day! It reminded me of everything that Mr. Marangakis told me in every detail about how God loves me. A question came to my mind: If God loves me, why did He let me get hurt? Why does a good god allow bad things to happen? But I told myself a good answer and said maybe it's something I don't understand. I came to terms with this question concluding that I didn't know everything.

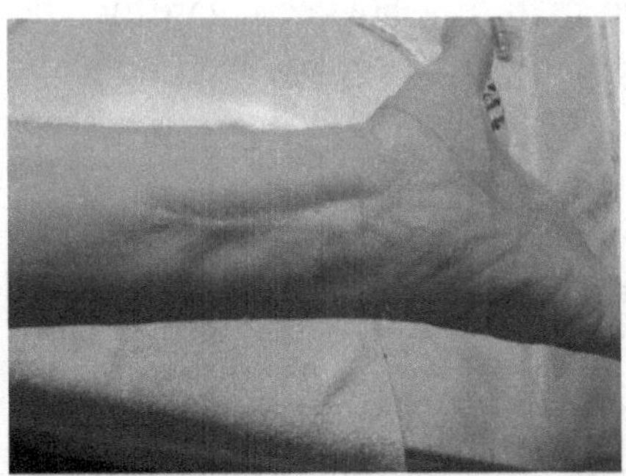

The scar on my left arm fifty-five years later

A week later they performed the second operation, restoring the skin over the wound. It was a nine-centimeter cut from the arm to the wrist. I could move all my fingers like before, and my hand would gain the same strength back over time. Fifty-five years later, the scar is there to remind me of God's healing grace. I began to believe when I was in the hospital that Jesus loves me and everything will be fine.

After two weeks I could stand and walk. After a month I wanted and was ready to return to my ship when it entered the port. I left with good memories of the hospital, thanks to the excellent care of the nurses and doctors. So I boarded the ship and stayed on board until March 1967. The captain and chief engineer gave me one month of sick leave and exemption from all work on the ship, which I liked so much, and the crew called me "Peter, the Tourist."

Then, together with my friend Odeseas, we returned to Rhodes, with enough money in our pockets from the work we did on the ship all these months. I hadn't written to my parents about the accident because I didn't want them to be sad. Meanwhile, my mother felt that something had happened to me, so she wrote to my friend

Odeseas, who told her about the accident. When I went to Rhodes, I gave them the gifts I had bought for my sisters, and when they saw how serious the cut on my arm was, they were shocked and very sad, as expected; but on the other hand, they thanked God that nothing worse happened. They were very happy that my hand was fully functional.

In the following months, I was urged by the Ministry of Merchant Marine to hire a lawyer regarding the accident because I could get some compensation for it. The ship-owning company paid the medical costs during my stay in the hospital, as well as two months' wages. I saw a lawyer of the company in Athens about the matter, and I would soon receive about 15,000 drachmas compensation, so I gave the lawyer my address there in Athens, where I was staying.

I now had some money from my work on board the ship and used it to enroll in a school in the city of Piraeus (Kotea and Milatos School—teachers of physics and mathematics) to prepare for the exams of the Ministry of Merchant Marine. The exams lasted three days and included six-hour written exams in physics, mathematics, geometry, trigonometry, steam and diesel engine operation, mechanical engineering, marine engineering, and English. I had to pass all these exams to become a third engineer officer in the merchant marine.

I rented a small room with a shared bathroom for three months in an old house in Pasalimani while studying for the exams. I paid three hundred drachmas a month. I cooked my own food and took great care of my expenses. But my main focus was to attend classes at the school and then study in the evening for the next day. Thank God, He gave me strength and persistence to complete the studies of all these subjects prior to the exam.

My money was almost over when the owner of the house I lived in asked me to pay rent in advance for the next three months. I couldn't do that, so I had to leave and find another place to stay. I found a very cheap hotel for twenty drachmas a day, and I agreed to pay at the end of each week. After moving into the hotel, I called the company's lawyer and gave them my new hotel address. I promised the hotel that I would pay for the room on Friday, not knowing how I would get the money. So I prayed to God about this situation.

That Friday I saw the hotel manager, and he gave me a surprise letter. I took it to my room and opened it. With tears in my eyes, I thanked God for the check of 15,000 drachmas (500 dollars) that I did not expect to come so soon! Payment came to me after court and lawyer's fees were paid. So I took the check to the bank, cashed it, and paid the hotel with a very happy smile on my face. I was rich! Out of joy I walked into a nearby restaurant, ordered a steak, and ate it with great pleasure.

Then I took the exams, which lasted three days, and waited for the results. A week later they were published. I read them on a sheet of paper placed on a telephone pole on the street in front of the ministry's offices (a very casual way of announcing results, but what mattered to me was that I passed, thank God!) After three months of hard study, it was so wonderful to hear that I had become a third engineer officer in the merchant marine. I felt so blessed!

I sent money to my parents in Rhodes and told them that I would soon board a new ship from the port of Piraeus with the rank of third engineer. I had a few more days to spend with my relatives in Athens. I finally had in my hands the diploma that I would present to the shipping companies for the new position.

My friend Odeseas joined the Greek army to fulfill his compulsory military service. I did not have to serve because, as I already mentioned, I was exempted from military service, due to being a refugee from Egypt's war.

PART 3

ON THE THIRD SHIP

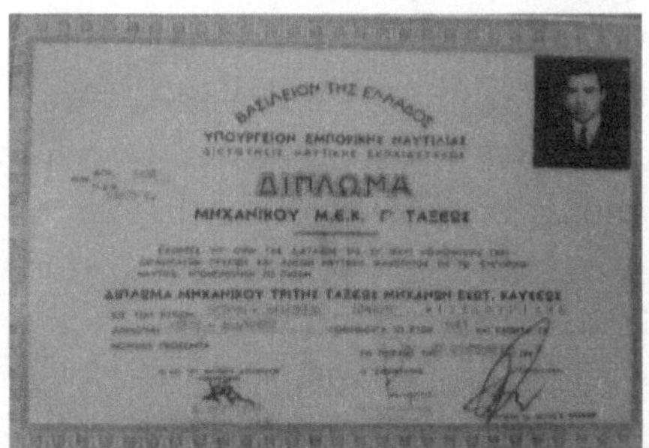

My diploma as a third engineer

Having in my hands the diploma of third engineer, full of joy and optimism, I went to the port of Piraeus and looked for work as an officer. In front of the office of the Merchant Marine building, there were lists of ships on which crew would be hired on a glass showcase. I found out that the company Livanos had available a ten-year-old ship named *Meandros*. I went to their office and applied, and they accepted me to work on their ship, which was in the Netherlands. After a week, the company paid my travel expenses, and I went with the rest of the crew to Rotterdam, Netherlands. It was a 25,000-ton ship carrying minerals and traveling to America, Africa, and Japan. The captain was from the island of Chios and was very good as a person and as a captain. The *Meandros* was a very beautiful ship. I had my own office, bedroom, and living room, which was air-conditioned with polished wooden floors. My library was full of engineering books on the engine and every other machine on board. I was so happy. I thanked God for this ship and the new job. I remember putting the Bible that Mr. Marangakis gave me in 1965 on the front of my desk. My joy was indescribable, that I would work as a third engineer! The new captain, thirty-two years old, was named Petros Paradisis. I was twenty-three years old at the time. Captain Paradisis was very fair, intelligent, and good with the crew, with a good sense of humor. I really liked him. I considered him my friend.

The ship was one of ten ships, built in Yugoslavia, of the Livanos Company. Five of them had Italian Fiat engines and the other five Sulzer engines, made in Switzerland. This ship was very well maintained and had a good crew, great facilities, air conditioning, all the paid overtime I wanted, and very good, fresh food.

My shift was from eight to twelve in the morning and eight to twelve in the evening. I learned so much every day, and I was very happy. We went to Africa, Japan, India, Pakistan, the coast of west Africa, Norfolk, Virginia, and New Orleans, transporting minerals to Japan and grain to India.

While I was on this ship, my dream of living in America grew stronger every day. Together with another officer of the bridge, Nikos Balabanis, twenty-seven years old, third captain from Chios and nephew of the captain, we decided to leave the ship the next time we arrived in America. My friend Nikos and I were planning to stay illegally in America when the time was right. He wanted to go to New York, and I wanted to go to Los Angeles. A few months earlier, we were in California in the summer of 1968, at the port of San Pedro, near the Port of Los Angeles. As usual, Mr. Marangakis came and took us once again to church. How happy I was when I saw again the beautiful and happy faces I met three years before! My friend Nikos and I wanted so badly to stay in Long Beach, but we didn't have the courage to leave the ship at that time.

In a café-bar in Long Beach, we met some Greeks who lived there in California and told us that they got their green cards (which means a permanent resident card to stay in the US) from "some guys" sitting there in the café-bar. We were told that for only 350 dollars, we could get our green cards and stay legally and permanently in America. I thought this was great and at a good price. We talked with them, and I decided to go there again at the next opportunity to meet them, while my friend Nikos would travel to New York to see some of his relatives. Although I knew this was not a legal way to stay in America, I decided to do it anyway. But if I had known the pain and danger I would face, I would never have done something like this. It would take us three months to put our plan into action.

In early October 1968, our ship docked in Portland, Oregon. Together with my friend Nikos, we said that this is the time, no more delays. We waited until the last day when the ship would depart to get off the ship so that we would not be searched for by the immigration office. The ship was due to leave the next morning, so we packed our bags, left the ship, and went straight to a hotel to spend the night. The next morning, we went to the airport. Nikos left for New York, and I left for Los Angeles. Before we separated, we promised each other that we would see each other after we settled down. Unfortunately, it was the last time I saw him. We shook hands, said goodbye, and each went our own way. With pain and tears in our hearts for separating from our best friend, we remained calm so as not to attract the attention of the airport officers. We boarded our separate planes and left.

I arrived in Los Angeles

I had the address of the middleman and decided to go see him, not realizing that I would be trapped in a very dangerous situation and would need God's intervention again to save me from the people with whom I would quickly get involved. I now was an illegal immigrant, and I was afraid that I would be discovered any day. I took a taxi and went straight to the house I had the address for. The contact person was there! Was I lucky? To my surprise, he asked me to pay him 350 dollars immediately. He told me that in just a few days, he would give me documents with which I could legally stay in America. I thought he would pay the fees to the Immigration Department to get me my green card. But I was fooled!

At the time, Los Angeles had thousands of hippies on the streets. Some of them used drugs and, in protest of the war in Vietnam, refused to be drafted. When I entered that house, I saw a lot of people inside. Many of them were drunk; some others didn't even know they were drunk. I smelled bad smoke and immediately knew that they didn't just smoke cigarettes. Some slept on the floor under the influence of the substances they smoked. How little did I realize that this would become a huge problem for me! Within days I learned that they were doing illegal transactions in this house. In the '60s, there were many such houses on almost every street. I agreed to pay every week in cash for my stay there, in addition to the money I had given to that guy to supposedly do my legal paperwork. I thought a week would be enough. But when I entered the house and saw those who lived there, I was afraid that I had made a very big mistake. Without knowing the language, without a driver's license or car, I was totally dependent on them.

A week later I asked them when they would prepare my papers. They kept postponing it, and I thought they would pay someone else to get the green card for legal stay.

I felt betrayed and that they had only used me to get my money. My worst fear was when I realized that the authorities would find out where I lived and, at any moment, come and arrest me. I am deliberately avoiding using names and details. I was also guilty, according to the law, as an accomplice (guilty by association) because I lived with them. Various guys came there from Mexico in very expensive cars. Very often I saw police officers in parked vehicles watching anyone entering or leaving the house. Sometimes, plainclothes police officers followed people entering the house and arrested them right there at the house.

The next two weeks, I was very scared because I saw a lot of illegal things happening in the house, and I wanted to leave; even my life was in danger. I tried to show them a friendly attitude by giving them some money to buy food. I had spent over a thousand dollars giving and lending nonrefundable loans to them. I was depressed, worried about my life, and had nowhere to go to ask for help. I felt so desperate! I wished I had never left my ship in Portland, and I was consumed by anxiety and fear as I lived among illegal and dangerous people.

I tried to pray. Then one night I remembered that in my bag I had a New Testament that Mr. Marangakis had given me three years ago. When he gave me the New Testament, he said to me, "Peter, do not sin. God loves you!" I had never heard these words in my life, and I always kept them in my heart like a hidden treasure. I opened the New Testament looking to read something that would give me some peace and certainty, and then I saw a phone number written inside! *Is it Mr. Marangakis's phone number?* I thought. I called him. A miracle! He answered the phone! Humbly, and embarrassed, I told him my problem in a few words, and he immediately offered to pick me up from there and take me to his house.

God led Mr. Marangakis to save me from this illegal group, and this would later result in my salvation in Christ. He came the same evening, after finishing his work at his restaurant, the Big Bun, and picked me up at 11:30 p.m. with his whole family in the car. We went to his house, and he said to me, "Peter, you will stay with us! I will be your father, my wife will be your mother, and my two sons will be your brothers. Tomorrow you will start working in the restaurant with me." He entrusted me with his family, home, and business! My heart broke in the face of such kindness, and I understood that this man was sent by God. To this day I have never seen such love from a Christian toward an unbelieving sinner. First time in a month and a half, I breathed free and safe. After a few days, we celebrated Christmas 1968 at his house, and I never saw anyone from that house again.

At Mr. Marangakis's house, I felt very safe and secure. Many times late at night, I would wake up and hear whispers in the living room. Walking fearfully on my tiptoes, I would walk down the hallway and look into the living room. I was surprised to see Mr. Marangakis in his pajamas praying on his knees in front of his couch. Because he did this so often, the couch had a dent where he rested his hands and head in prayer.

A month later, Mr. Marangakis found me an extra job in a machine shop in El Monte, on Rush Street (A&B Tool and Die), owned by a Greek, Mr. Nikos Arvanitis from Athens, who listened to my story with compassion and promised that he would get me an invitation to come to the United States since he could obtain the required legal documents so that I could work as a technician in his business.

It was in this factory that I met my good friend, Themis Katsaros, from Ikaria. He was an honest and intelligent engineer. It didn't take long for us to become good friends. He told me that he was engaged to a beautiful girl who lived in Athens and that he would soon go there to marry her. He asked about my past, and I told him my story. I told him that I was in America illegally and if it wasn't for Mr. Marangakis, I would have been in big trouble. I also talked to him about the beautiful experiences I had with people in Mr. Marangakis's church. Themis was very interested and wanted to hear more about this new Greek church and what was spoken from the Bible there.

In the following months, with the help of Mr. Marangakis, I got a driver's license and bought a used car to go to work and church. I was very careful not to break the law because the Immigration Department was still looking for me. Now, my life was getting much better, working in the machine shop by day and in the restaurant by night and enjoying socializing with the faithful people of the Greek Apostolic Church of Los Angeles. I remember taking Mr. Marangakis's sons, Chris and Tim, to the youth meetings at church with my car.

THE GREATEST
EVENT OF MY LIFE

The various experiences I had all these months culminated in a big event that took place on the weekend of July 4, 1969. I thought that one day I, too, would become a good Christian, like the people who loved me in the church I attended. The purpose of my life was to start a family and live the beautiful life of the American Dream with my own efforts. How wrong I was! Every perfect gift comes from above, from our heavenly Father, the Father of lights, in whom there is no alteration or shadow of change. Man can only change the exterior, but God can change everything by giving us a new heart. And that hadn't happened to me yet.

It was Sunday night, and I was listening in church to Pastor Nick Tunger from the San Francisco Greek Assembly who was unknown to me. His message about the love of Christ pierced my heart and convicted me deeply of my sins. For the first time in my life, I realized that I had to believe that Jesus accepts me, that He forgives my sins and wants to make me His child. When the message was finished, the minister, evangelist Charlie Cancillas from Los Angeles, called us to pray. I had never felt such a touch in my heart. I stepped forward, knelt down, and prayed for over an hour with tears in my eyes. When I got up, I knew something great had happened in my life because the joy and freedom I felt was something unique and unprecedented for me. I knew that Jesus was my Savior, who took away all my fears and all my sins. I felt that I was a young person full of heavenly joy, something I had been asking for all my life. A young girl at church asked me if I was born again. I had never heard this phrase, but it was the best description of my new situation. Yes, everything became new! Above all, Jesus was my Savior. From that moment on, I belonged to God, my heavenly Father, and every day since then, that joy has grown, even to this day.

When I had that terrible accident three years ago on the ship, which almost cost me my life, God protected me, and while I was semiconscious, a sweet voice had said to me, "You will not die, but something great will happen to you!" Well, that same voice spoke into my ear that night and said, "This is the great thing that was going to happen to you." It was my salvation in Christ Jesus that happened to me! Jesus redeemed me and forgave my sins by giving me grace and mercy because He loves me. I was so excited that night! I felt like I was thirsty and someone gave me a river of water. I felt like I was hungry and a good friend who owns a restaurant gave me all the food I wanted. I felt like I was falling into a dark mess and a strong and tender hand grabbed me, put me in His arms, and took me to His light. The joy I felt was so overwhelming and wonderful! Jesus told me that this kind of joy comes only from heaven.

Later that night when I got home, I had a foretaste of heaven! It was around eleven or twelve, and I was getting ready for bed because I was going to work in the morning. I felt so blessed and happy! I was so excited, laughing and trembling in prayer on my knees, enthralled by God's great love for me. At one point, I took the alarm clock while on my knees next to the bed and was winding it up to set it for 6:00 a.m. to go to work when suddenly the alarm went off while it was still in my hand! I thought I had set it wrong, but when I looked up and saw the light coming in through the window, it was already dawn. I was amazed! I stood up and felt refreshed and ready for the new day, without having slept at all! Those six or seven hours of kneeling and experiencing the blessing of God's presence seemed to be only one minute! Perhaps God used those hours for me to experience eternity with Him. I felt as if I had gone *from darkness to light* within minutes.

I got dressed for work and left happy and excited. Entering the machine shop with this newfound joy in my heart, Mr. Arvanitis noticed a difference in my face and said, "Peter, something happened to you!" I told him that God made me a new man. At 9:00 a.m., I asked Mr. Arvanitis if I could go to Disneyland to meet the group of kids from the church who were going there. He gave me permission and told me that I can make up the hours on Saturday.

Disneyland in Anaheim, California

When I arrived at Disneyland, I was surprised to see that in front of the entrance, there was a huge parking lot with thousands of cars, while I had the impression that it would only be a small park. I went to the gate and bought a ticket. I told the clerk that I needed to find my friends who were inside, and he asked me if it was an emergency. They could call for them over the intercom to meet me. I was about to say it was an emergency, but then I thought I couldn't lie. I began to remember all the lies I had told in the past, including the fact that I came to America legally. Something inside me had changed and I knew lying was a sin and I chose not to lie anymore and I didn't want to. So I told the clerk it wasn't an emergency, and he said, "Good luck! Find them yourself." I entered and got lost among forty-five thousand people. How could I find my twenty friends in this crowd?

Ice-cream cart

After wandering around for a while and getting lost, I remembered God and asked Him to help me find them. I went to an ice-cream cart and bought twenty ice creams. I sat on a nearby bench, closed my eyes, and prayed. Then, looking up after praying, I saw my twenty friends pass in front of me! They were so happy to see me and took the ice cream because it was very hot that day. My heavenly Father showed me the way like a little child so that I would not get lost. He held my hand and guided me each day with new thoughts and amazing revelations about life with Him. My friends asked me how I found them. I told them I was just praying, and when I opened my eyes, they were there in front of me. It was an unforgettable day, spent with newfound Christian friends.

After the Disneyland experience, I got into the daily routine: going to prayer at church on Wednesday night, gathering with the young people on Friday night, and going to church on Sunday. I was a new car driver, but I made the trip from home to work and church very often. Chris and Tim Marangakis often went with me around town and church. They liked my jokes, and with my broken English, I told them things that made them laugh. They called me "big brother."

One evening, as Chris, Tim, and I were returning from church to their parents' restaurant and covering a distance of about twenty miles, the steering wheel of the car began to shake and vibrate in an unusual way. Arriving at the restaurant, I stopped in the parking lot and tried the steering wheel by turning it left and then right. It was spinning each way freely! I opened the hood of the car and looked inside with a flashlight. The steering shaft was broken, and there was no connection to the wheels. If this had happened five minutes earlier, we would have had no way to control the car on the highway and we would have crashed or worse. We were speechless! God protected us again (another miracle). It was an old '59 Buick Wildcat with tires worn out from years of use.

'59 Buick Wildcat

A few days later, after the miraculous event with the broken steering wheel, I felt uncomfortable because I was in America illegally. I knew I had to do something about it. I asked Mr. Marangakis to take me to the Immigration Department and I would surrender. I could no longer live a lie. So he took me to their offices in downtown Los Angeles, and they arrested me. They were surprised that I surrendered and asked why I did it. I told them that I was a Christian and could no longer live in a lie and that God was in control of my life. For this reason, they gave me a month to stay in America, and if I did not leave the country at my own expense by then, they would send me back to Greece by deportation. They asked Mr. Marangakis to leave, and they put me in jail while investigating my case for two days.

I felt God's presence beside me. I gladly expected God to do something beautiful every day. He had surprised me so many times and shown me His loving care and protection, so I was optimistic. Those two days in prison in Los Angeles were very difficult. The guards were very harsh with the prisoners, and I was very afraid. On the morning of the third day, I was released and called Mr. Marangakis to come and get me. He was so kind; he came to the center and took me home. God bless him for his selfless acts of kindness.

After a few days, Mr. Arvanitis, along with a lawyer and Mr. Marangakis, decided to go to the Immigration Department and apply for my legal entrance to America for me. We were told that I had to go through a hearing because I had committed a violation of the law and that the judge would decide whether to accept or reject the application for a legal return. The law said that if I left the United States voluntarily and at my own expense, the violation of the law would be deleted. In the end, the conclusion of the investigation stated that I had not committed any other violation of the law.

Mr. Nikolas Arvanitis—technician, inventor, and poet

A few days later, I went with Mr. Arvanitis at 9:00 a.m. for the hearing before a judge at the Immigration Department in downtown Los Angeles. With us was Mr. Marangakis and the lawyer hired by Mr. Arvanitis. The judge asked me, "Why did you confess to the Immigration Department about illegally leaving the ship?" I answered that I was "born again" and could no longer live a lie. The judge said, "I've heard this before!" After asking me the question, he rested his head on the palm of his hand and fell asleep! All four of us were puzzled to watch him sleep with his head resting in one hand for about a minute! At that point, the lawyer stepped forward and handed the petition to the judge and asked him to sign it. The judge was still asleep. Mr. Marangakis told us softly in Greek, "Our God has put him to sleep!" The judge opened his eyes and said, "Where should I sign?" The lawyer took the signed document, and we all left quietly but hurriedly out of the courtroom. The judge had approved my legal return through the Immigration Division!

We left the court excited and overjoyed! God was again showing me that His hand was on me. I was so happy that my dreams would come true! I could legally immigrate to America! Of course, it would still take months to complete the process, but it was the beginning of fulfilling my dream. I had one month of accommodation to get ready and leave the country.

I couldn't leave and go to Canada or Mexico to get a visa for the United States since I didn't have a passport. So I continued to work in the machine shop, pay my bills and rent, and prepare for the last day of my extension, which they had given me as a favor. In the meantime, Mr. Arvanitis arranged for me to get a new passport to be issued through a travel agent working with the Greek Embassy in San Francisco. I gave him all my necessary details, and I knew it would take a long time because the embassy would have to contact Greece to verify this information. I worked two jobs to earn enough money to take with me when I left. One was in a restaurant on Florence Avenue, next to a car wash, shared by Mr. David, who was Jewish Greek, and Mr. Nikos Valaskatzis. I worked in Mr. Arvanitis's factory until four in the afternoon, and then in the restaurant at five in the afternoon until two in the morning. Then I would return to El Monte and sleep until 6:00 a.m. and then back to Mr. Arvanitis's machine shop. That's what I did every day for a month. Both my employers in the restaurant were serious businessmen and gentlemen, and they respected me as a Christian. I only had three hours to sleep each night.

On the way home at 2:00 a.m., I was so tired that I often closed my eyes while driving and only woke up when I heard tires go over the dividers in the middle of the road. Every night I saw hundreds of trucks with military equipment going down to the docks to bring weapons for the Vietnam War. One day, on my way to work in the restaurant from the machine shop, I fell asleep from fatigue. Although I was driving at twenty to thirty miles per hour, I did not have time to apply the brakes and hit a stopped car in front of me driven by a lady. We got out of our cars, and she asked me, "Why didn't you stop?" I apologized to her and told her it was my fault. We both called our insurances, who took care of the cost of the damage, but the problem was that I didn't have a car to go back to work in the evening!

Then I was surprised by another fact. The owner of the restaurant, Mr. David, temporarily gave me his car, knowing that I would leave at the end of the month. It was a brand-new 1968 Toyota model, and he told me I could keep it as long as I wanted. He was so nice to me. Mr. Nikos trusted me because I went to the Greek Apostolic Church in Los Angeles. He wanted someone he could trust to close the shop and save the cash from the register. So I hid the money in a bag and put it under the barrel of pickles so that he could get it in the morning, when he came to the store. I would go to both jobs over the next few weeks until I left. I paid the insurance company for the damage to the lady's car. I said goodbye to Mr. Nikos and Mr. David on the last day before I left and told them that I had no way to leave the country because I had no passport and I knew that if I was arrested, I would be deported.

A week before I left, Mr. Arvanitis, as I mentioned a little before, had contacted a Greek who owned a travel agency who applied for a Greek passport for me. The passport came by post to the machine shop the same day I had to leave! I was surprised they sent it so soon! It was validated by the Greek Embassy in San Francisco, but it was too late to use it because, to apply in Canada or Mexico and get their approval, it would take months, and there was no time to do it because I had to leave that same day.

It was the end of the month, and I was a little scared about what the day had in store for me. I had my suitcase with a few things inside next to me by the machine I was working on in the machine shop and waited. It was the last day that I had to leave the country voluntarily; otherwise, I would be arrested.

A SMALL MIRACLE AGAIN, AT THE LAST MINUTE

At 10:30 a.m., the phone rang in the machine shop. It was Captain Themos from the company Livanos based on the west coast, Portland, Oregon, on the phone. He asked me if I wanted to return to the ship where I worked, the *Meandros. Did he make fun of me, knowing it was my last day, or was it a miracle again?* I wondered. I didn't think he was who he said he was. He got angry on the phone and told me that he didn't have time for jokes but that he wanted to know if I would go back to the ship that was arriving in Portland that night. He knew where I worked because the Immigration Department had contacted him. He told me that the ship would dock that night and I could return to the same ship and port where I had left about ten months ago. He told me to go to Los Angeles Airport, where they would have a ticket ready for me to fly to Portland, Oregon, with TWA.

I called Mr. Marangakis, who happened to be home, and told him that the captain of the ship I was working on before called me and told me that he had a ticket ready at the airport for me to go to Oregon and join his crew again. "Didn't I tell you that God is with you?" he said. In an hour he came to the machine shop with his wife, Dolly, and his two sons, Chris and Tim, to take me to the airport. I told them that I had paid all my bills and my rent. This man had saved me from the bad company I was involved in, found me a job, brought me to church, where I accepted Jesus Christ as my Savior, and finally, along with his family, brought me to the airport to leave for Portland. I said goodbye to all my colleagues in the machine shop. My friend, Themis, had gone to Greece to get married.

In an hour we were at Los Angeles Airport. I hugged and kissed the Marangakis family one by one and then got on the plane. There were no security checks that would delay my entry. I thanked them all warmly for their love and prayers, and they assured me that together with the whole church, they would pray for me to return as soon as possible. I prayed the same! In half an hour the plane would depart.

I sat on the plane, and looking out the window, I spotted Mr. Marangakis and his family waving goodbye to me. They couldn't see me, but I looked at them with emotion and wept in gratitude for God's providence through their love and care for me. But I was afraid that it might be the last time I would see them, and that brought sadness to my heart. Although God only knows tomorrow, God loves us today and tomorrow.

After an hour and a half, the plane arrived in Portland, Oregon. As I was getting off the plane, I noticed someone holding a big sign with my name on it to take me by taxi to the port. We first went to the shipping company's office, and I signed some papers with Captain Themos, commodore of the west coast fleet for the Livanos Company. I asked if Captain Paradisis was on board and if he really wanted me to return. I was ashamed to face him. I had tricked him when I left the ship and wondered if he had forgiven me or not. They told me that the captain wants me back and that he will promote me to second engineer! I didn't believe what they were saying. How could a seafarer who left the ship be accepted back and be promoted? But they assured me that the captain likes me and wants me back.

In the meantime, I was warned by the Immigration Department that I would be arrested if I was not on the boat no later than midnight because it was the last day of the month of the extension. Around 11:30 p.m. the ship arrived at the port. The captain had received the message that I was at the dock and had accepted the terms of return to the ship. All the old crew and some new ones were on the upper deck, at the front of the ship, waiting with interest to see the sailor returning to the ship, from which he had left to remain in America. They thought I was a fool for coming back. Others vilified me, while others told me that my engine room was waiting for me.

Overall, however, they were all waiting curiously to hear my story about my ten-month adventure in Los Angeles.

I had learned to speak a little better English over the past few months and could communicate better with the people on the dock who were waiting with me. I shared with them my testimony of how Jesus saved me, and they listened to me. I knew God was with me, and as I waited for the ship to sail, I thanked God from the bottom of my heart for His loving care. Yes, Jesus Christ was now my Savior and Lord. A few minutes before midnight, I was on the ship without fear of deportation. It was another miracle. I laughed with tears of joy as I had lost count of the many miracles that had happened to me.

I went straight to the bridge of the ship and saw Captain Petros Paradisis. He embraced me with great joy. With tears in my eyes, I asked him to forgive me. He asked me why I behaved so foolishly, leaving the ship so secretly and quickly, and told me that he would have helped me to do it in a better way. He also told me that the second engineer would return to Greece in a few weeks and that I would replace him with a promotion in his position! Now I know from personal experience that when God forgives you, He will also make people forgive you—like immigration offices, captains, chief engineers, west coast CEO of the company, etc.! But I also learned that as God forgives me, I need to forgive others.

In Portland, the ship unloaded, and we went north to Washington and loaded timber and grain. Then we sailed south, passing through the Panama Canal, and continued to the Atlantic Ocean. I was in the officers' dining room and bowed my head to pray. Seeing me, the officers in the dining room thought I was stupid or joking. I told them I was thanking God for the food and for bringing me back to the ship. They told me I was a fool to come back on board. Of course, they did not use the word *fool*.

I was with this crew for a few weeks as we traveled to Italy. They saw my new life and understood that I was truly a changed person. They knew me before, and now I was different. I treated everyone with kindness and spoke with love and respect to the entire crew, from the chief engineer to the janitors. I told them about God many times. I would gather them in my office and share my stories with them. I brought with me on board a small suitcase with New Testaments, like the one Mr. Marangakis had given me three and a half years ago that Christmas morning. Surprisingly, I did the same thing he did with the Greek sailors in the ports. Those who wanted to know more, I invited them to my office for a Bible study. To my surprise, many wanted to come and hear what I had to say.

As third engineer on the third ship

Peter in the engine room

During the time I was on the previous two ships, I remember that when I woke up, my tongue had marks from its intense pressure against my teeth due to anxiety and fear of the ship sinking. We passed through wild storms with waves of ten meters and feared for our lives many times when the weather was so bad. We thought we were going to die, not knowing where we were going. But on this ship now when I woke up, my tongue wasn't marked like that. I slept calm and peaceful, thinking of all the good things God had done for me and all the good people I had met in America. I knew God wanted me back on my ship, but I was sad because I missed the sweet company of the brothers at the Los Angeles church.

I was very kind to my crew and regretted that it was often too hot in their cabins. So I allowed them to come into my cabin, which had air conditioning, and sleep on the floor. When I returned from my shift, I would often grab a pillow and sleep on the floor as well. Some of the officers told me that what I was doing was not right and that I had to keep my distance from the crew. But I was now a Christian and felt compassion for my crew. And when I gave them my testimony, they accepted it.

Of course, not everything was beautiful on board. I had some friction with the second captain who didn't like me saying, "Now I'm a Christian." He would say, "What are you talking about? We are all Christians!" He thought I was pretending. He threw into my cabin windows periodicals with dirty photos for the crew to see. He denied that he did it, but my crew knew what kind of person he was and didn't doubt me at all. However, he saw that I was kind and that I prayed for everyone who came knocking on my door, asking for prayer, because they were afraid of the storms, especially the younger crew.

I believe it was God who gave me the wonderful idea to help the crew paint the ship's holds. Captain Minas was in charge of the crew for cleaning and maintaining the metal walls of the ship. The inner walls of the holds had to be cleaned, scraped, primed, and then sprayed with metallic paint. The workers wore only an ordinary mask, and because the cleaning materials were very caustic, they could not stay there for more than ten minutes, so they had to stop and go up to the deck to get fresh air. Many fainted or vomited from the strong, toxic odors they inhaled. So, seeing the inadequate protective equipment they were using, I decided to help them.

I designed a way so that the air pump connected to the paint can have a two-way channel for air: one channel for spraying the paint and one for the face mask so that it sends fresh air to the nasal area but also has holes for the exit of air under the eyes so that the paint does not get into the mask and keeps it clean and clear. The second channel needed a reducer to make air enter the mask at a slower pressure. It was an amazing invention, and the captain said he would send the idea to headquarters for patenting.

However, the second captain, Minas, did not want to accept my idea and went down to the hold without a mask, to prove that my idea was foolish and unnecessary. But, after a few minutes, he fainted from the fumes! They had to lift him out with ropes and put him on his bed. He had bleeding ulcers in the stomach and coughing. He was very sick. I brought him some soup from the kitchen and prayed for him. He then disembarked from the ship at the next port and was sent to his home in Athens for recovery. Before leaving the ship, he confessed that he had put those dirty magazines in my room. I told him I knew it from the beginning. "And yet you cared about me?" he asked me. "Yes," I replied. When he left the ship, he thanked me for taking care of him and praying for him, and he was very sorry for all the inconvenience he caused me by throwing the magazines into my room.

From the first week of my return to the ship, I began teaching my crew in my cabin from the New Testament. Many young men came with drawers from their cabins and used them as desks and seats. I didn't know much of the Bible, but something amazing began to happen. When they asked me a question about something, I would open my Bible, and my eyes would fall on the page with the correct answer, and I would learn with them! I taught them all to say the Lord's Prayer, but I told them that they could pray and speak to God in their own words as well. They were surprised to hear this.

PROBLEMS IN THE ATLANTIC OCEAN

Some amazing things happened in these months, and I saw in all of them again the hand of God. Traveling east to Italy, in the Atlantic Ocean, we were faced with a very fierce storm. In such a case, we are not allowed to walk on deck. Many of the vertical protective railings surrounding the ship were broken because they had been damaged by the waves. Something even worse happened during this terrible storm. The base of the radio antenna, which was mounted on the top of the mast, broke due to the strong winds and waves. The ship's communication system depended on this antenna, and we were in danger without it. The captain, along with the chief engineer and myself, made a plan for its urgent repair. The storm had calmed down a bit, but it was still very dangerous. So we all decided that I would climb to the top of the mast and repair the broken antenna by welding the base to the mast. I don't remember how tall the mast was, but it was very tall. Worst of all, I was afraid of heights and would get dizzy up there.

I went to my room and prayed. Then we transferred the welding machine from the engine room to the base of the mast. I tied one welding wire with one pole, around my waist, and fixed the other pole to the base of the mast. Every half meter I climbed up the mast, I asked God to be with me and remove fear while the ship tilted sometimes to the right and sometimes to the left. As I climbed higher, I could see the ocean stretching from side to side while the ship was rocking all the time. I tried not to look down on the deck and told myself that fear is just an emotion, but that didn't help much. I kept asking Jesus to keep me safe. There was a danger that the rail around the mast would break due to my weight. As I climbed, I was pulling a very heavy copper welding cord tied to my waist. In addition to this, I also had a second rope tied to my waist with tools, in case I needed them. In fear, I wondered if I had done the right thing to return to the ship and volunteer for this dangerous job.

Eventually, I reached the top of the mast and had to scrape the paint off its base to be able to weld the antenna to the small steel platform just as I had done down at the base of the mast. At the top of the mast, there was a large circular base about a meter in diameter, and I sat on it to catch my breath and relax. That was the scariest experience of my life. After I welded the antenna correctly and the engineers underneath told me that everything seemed okay and was vertically straight, I untied the rope and cable from my waist and let it fall to the deck. I slowly came down to the deck one step at a time. The electrician now had to climb up to connect the wires to the antenna. At the base of the mast, I knelt down and thanked God for His protection and the success of this difficult and dangerous undertaking. To this day, I am still afraid of heights, and I know full well that He was the one who helped me this time too.

Meanwhile, another incident occurred. We had a big problem in the engine room with cylinder 2 of the main engine. While at sea, we discovered a crack in the engine cylinder and had to remove the piston along with the connecting rod and then the cylinder. It was very dangerous work as we were in the ocean without an engine. Fortunately at this time, we did not have a storm. We had to detach the cylinder head, the piston, and the cylinder itself using a large electric and overhead crane of the engine room. While moving the crane, which had the piston and connecting rod hooked onto it, I had to bring the crane over to an opening on the first floor of the engine room and then lower the piston into the opening.

Twenty-foot piston rod

While the piston rod was in the air, with a dozen or so people below watching, the crane and braking system stopped working. The piston began to descend, without interruption and without us being able to control its movement. Even the cylinder brakes of the steel cable did not work. Thus, control systems were useless. The twenty-foot piston rod was coming down uncontrolled, away from the opening it was supposed to go into, while we had people underneath, putting them all in danger. Suddenly, I felt God's strength come upon me, and I shouted for everyone to run away. I grabbed the piston rod and tried to push it toward the opening that was a meter away. With all my strength and without fear, I pushed it into the opening. The piston rod did not go in straight but was stuck at an angle in the opening and held. Only the end of the piston rod was in the opening. The hook holding the piston rod descended with the steel cable uncontrollably. To our surprise, the piston rod that was stuck at an angle in the opening did not fall. Eventually, the electrician came and replaced the fuse and was able to reconnect all the wires and raise the piston safely for repair. Unless you were there at the time, it is very difficult to understand this very dangerous condition on board. With a repaired crane, we lifted the piston and placed it in the hole in the correct position, and then replaced the cylinder and everything else needed. It took about twelve hours to repair. When all was completed, we started up the engine, and it ran like new. And, thank God, no one was harmed.

Going to Italy

The captain told me that they had hired about eight to ten new sailors, among them was my brother George, and that we would pick them up in Italy when we arrived at the port. My young brother would work on the ship as an apprentice engineer. There in Italy, I officially become a second engineer. I was responsible for all the mechanics and instruments of the ship, as well as the safety of the crew, lifeboats, and disaster training. I had an office in my cabin and a library with books for the maintenance of the ship. My floor was covered with carpet and was air-conditioned and cleaned daily. My clothes were also brought to me clean. The walls were metal, very warm, when we traveled to the tropics.

My brother George, who I hadn't seen for many years, spent a lot of time together with me after he came on board with the new crew. I told him all my adventures in America, and he told me about our family in Greece. He also told me about our sisters' weddings, which, unfortunately, I could not attend. We had a great time together. I was surprised how good an engineer my brother was. Every job he did in the engine room was perfect.

In the spring of the following year, 1970, while on my ship, I received the documents approving Mr. Arvanitis's application from the United States Department of Justice inviting me to immigrate to the United States. They asked me which embassy I wanted my paperwork to be forwarded to, to get my visa, and I chose Vancouver, Canada.

I was now very excited, and with my documents in hand, I was ready to leave the ship and travel to Canada as a future immigrant to the United States! But there would be one more trial or challenge to face before leaving the ship as second engineer!

MY LAST JOB ON BOARD WAS NOT IN THE ENGINE ROOM!

We were waiting outside the port in Amsterdam, Holland, and received a message to lift the anchor and go to the dock to unload. The second captain gave the order to raise the anchor. Raising the anchor requires a very special technique to be done correctly. The pulling of long chains with the winch must be done slowly until the anchors reach the ship; otherwise, if done abruptly, there is a risk that they will get wedged in the tapered holes of the ship. Unfortunately, this was not done correctly that day with the left anchor. It was accidentally pulled with great force and wedged into the hole. They tried to get it out, but it was impossible. In this situation, we docked the ship and unloaded the cargo in three to four days. I was preparing to leave the ship when I finished this work, and I gladly thanked God that I was now on a legal return trip to America.

That night the captain and chief engineer again asked me to help them remove the anchor that had been wedged. I told them I would leave the next morning. They told me they couldn't leave the dock unless both anchors worked. The next morning several crew members were hitting the anchor from inside the ship, but the anchor was stuck too deep in the ship's tapered hole and would not come out.

I prayed that God would help us and put on my overalls. I took my crew and got to work. We hung with ropes a wooden platform on the side of the ship near the anchor and, sitting on it, proceeded to weld plates to the anchor and the ship, so as to place hydraulic jacks between the two plates. When the pressure of the hydraulic jacks increased, the space between the two plates opened, and inch by inch we slowly moved the anchor. However, when the anchor was released and floated into the void, there was a risk that it would crush me by hitting me against the ship. That's why I had a rope tied around my waist so that the sailors on the upper deck could hold me and quickly pull me up before the anchor would swing and hit the ship. That was the plan, and thank God, it worked. After two hours of hydraulic pumping and adding a washer to the distance between the two plates, the anchor was released. The sailors on the upper deck quickly pulled me and kept me safe as the anchor fell. Then all of them burst into applause and shouted excitedly, while I thanked God from the bottom of my heart that I would be able to see America without broken bones! Even the Dutch dockers, watching on the dock, applauded when the anchor was freed, and the sailors quickly hoisted me up safely. Anyone who does not know the size and weight of these anchors and the fastenings of large ships will never understand the huge danger I went through, especially when the anchor swayed freely toward the ship.

It was late July 1970 that I left the ship, with the permission and blessing of the captain this time, from Amsterdam, Netherlands, and departed by plane for Montreal, Canada. Crossing Canada by train, I arrived after three days in Vancouver, where I stayed three months for a background investigation by the American Embassy on Georgia Street. When the investigation was completed, in late October 1970, I was given a visa and legally entered the United States on November 1, 1970!

But I needed money to support myself for those three months in Canada (rent, food, paperwork, embassy translations), so I worked in a tile factory somewhere in the city. I had to load heavy tiles into boxes from a production belt. The job was very difficult for my back. I had to lift five heavy tiles in half a minute from a loading zone and put them in a box, eight hours a day. My back hurt, and my fingers very often bled. I worked in this factory for about two months.

One day, while I was at the US Embassy to check on the progress of my paperwork, I met a Greek man who had come to get a visa and go to the United States to see his sister who was sick, but they were making it difficult for him for various reasons that I do not want to mention. I encouraged him and prayed for him. In a couple of days, the embassy changed their mind and decided to give him a visa! He was so grateful and happy that he gave me his car for free (1963, Studebaker). It was an amazing and economical car made in Canada, and I wish I had kept it all these years. It looked like a little Mercedes. So, within days of this incident, I was authorized to legally immigrate to the United States and had a car to drive there as well. God showed me day by day that He loved and cared for me. And I always remember Him saying, "Peter, God loves you."

The free car (Studebaker 1963)

NEW BEGINNING IN AMERICA SINCE NOVEMBER 1970

On November 1, 1970, I left Vancouver, Canada, and drove south on the I-5 to the United States. My heart overflowed with gratitude for God's goodness as I realized that my dream of living in the country I loved had been fulfilled. About half an hour after crossing the border, I stopped at the border patrol building, and an officer came out and checked my pass. I gave him the yellow envelope that the embassy had given me. The officer opened it and took out my papers and green card. He said to me in broken Greek, *"Kalos oreses stien Ameriki!"* ("Welcome to America!") These were the sweetest words I ever heard from an American officer. I wanted to hug him and kiss him out of joy! God answered my heart's prayers and desire to live in America!

As I drove south, to the left of the highway, there was a tall, snowy mountain. I couldn't continue my drive because tears of gratitude to God started clouding my vision, and I remember stopping on the right side of the road. I walked a little through the forest, knelt down, and started crying, thanking God for His blessings on my life. Full of joy now, I continued my journey, and in three days, I arrived in Los Angeles. I went straight to Mr. Marangakis's house. When I arrived at his house, no one was there. Then I remembered that it was Wednesday and that he was at church for the evening service. I parked my car and waited for them to come home. As I waited for them, I had a few thoughts and said prayers to God, prayers of thanksgiving for so many good people who helped me get to this point in my life and fulfill my dream. I was amazed at why I was so happy, and then my heart told me the reason for my happiness is only one word: Jesus!

Without Christ, the forest becomes a desert without water. With Christ, the dry desert becomes a forest of trees full of fruit.

> You make known to me the path of life; you
> will fill me with joy in your presence, with eternal
> pleasures at your right hand. (Psalm 16:11 NIV)

Now, I say with sadness, in my old country no priest had ever told me that God loves me! Instead, they performed a routine liturgy, chanting in ancient Greek, and no one understood what they were saying. If you had the courage to ask a priest or a theologian a question, they would say, "Shame on you for asking! Don't search, just believe." However, if there is an eternity ahead of us, we should investigate and learn about it while we are still alive. Here on earth is the only chance. I wanted to ask many questions and find answers to the true meaning of life, but neither in schools nor in churches did anyone tell me how to receive eternal life. They said I had to learn about eternity and choose where I wanted to be when I left this world. Thank God, I found the answers I was looking for, not in America but in Christ who led someone to speak to me. I chose to believe in God and His Son Jesus Christ as my Lord and Savior, but with God's help. I say that I found Christ, but this is not correct because Christ was not lost and had to be found; I was lost, so Christ found me. Christ is everywhere, and His Word must be taught to everyone everywhere. Jesus spoke to all, and today He still speaks to everyone through His words in the Gospels. For He alone is the way, the truth, and the life. No one goes to heaven except through Him.

I remember when I was a little kid, I was eager to come to America. I remember the American sailors who had come to Rhodes and hired me to prepare and serve them sandwiches while they were playing baseball in the fields on the island. It was the first time I saw soft white bread, American cheese, salami and ham, mayonnaise and pickles. They were so nice and kind to me! I would prepare the sandwiches and put some on the side to take home for my family, and they would pay me for my help with silver coins! I was twelve to thirteen years old. The Sixth Fleet of the US Navy made many stops on our island. The names of those navy ships I remember were USS *Forrestal*, USS *Salem* aircraft carriers, and USS *Enterprise* (first nuclear aircraft carrier). When I was attending the school in Rhodes, we visited the USS *Enterprise*. We saw most of the ship, except for the protected areas, where the nuclear engine room was. The doors to the nuclear engine room were closed, and guards with guns were in front of these doors, mainly to demonstrate the safety of the nuclear engine rooms.

When Mr. Marangakis returned home with his family that night, I met them at the front of the house, where they welcomed me with love and tears of joy. The next day, after settling my suitcase in the small new apartment, I went straight to A&B Tool and Die to see Mr. Arvanitis in the machine shop. They welcomed me there with hugs and kisses and welcomed me with great joy. I expressed my appreciation for his efforts in inviting me as a legal immigrant to the United States. I had to work in his machine shop for at least six months to fulfill immigration requirements. I hugged my friend Themis and started telling him my news from my return to the ship and every adventure I had since the last time I saw him. I was pleased to see that he was asking me more about the Bible and thirsty to learn more about God.

Mr. Arvanitis, wearing the boss's "hat" and with a wide smile, told me to stop talking because there was a lot of work at that time that needed to be done quickly. "I don't pay you to talk, but to work," he told us. He had signed many contracts with the government in connection with the war in Vietnam, so his machine shop worked nonstop. Mr. Arvanitis was a good engineer, designer, and inventor, but most of his time was spent writing poems and checking our work. My friend Themis Katsaros, who had recently married, was the most meticulous mechanic and tool maker I have ever met in my life, as well as an amazing artist who painted Greek landscapes in great detail. It was a special privilege for me to have Themis as my friend.

I must mention here that when I went to church the following Wednesday night, I had the clear assurance that God wanted me to come much closer to Him because He had a special ministry for me in relationship to these beautiful people whom I loved so much. This made me scared because I couldn't speak in public without stuttering. I was much more afraid to question this affirmation that clearly came from God.

Meanwhile, my friend Themis had gone to Greece and married his fiancée, Koula. He had brought her from Greece, and they were staying here in Alhambra. After a few weeks of working in the machine shop, he invited me to go meet his wife. I went to their apartment and enjoyed a nice dinner. She was a beautiful girl who had a great love for Themis. Themis had asked me not to tell her anything more about my new life in Christ because he didn't know how she would react. She was very educated and very intelligent, but I saw in her eyes how thirsty she was for the truth. Themis had accepted everything I had told him about the Lord and had shared it with her before I came. I respected his will and said nothing about the Bible in those first few days with her.

Themis and Koula, my friends forever

Every time we met, she was curious and full of questions for me. I answered her with love and respect. I didn't want to offend what she believed or didn't. The life a Christian lives in front of people is the best preaching. People will have doubts about what we say, but not about what we do. I had gained a little experience on board the ship as a young Christian. I had made many mistakes in talking to others about God, offending their traditional beliefs, written or unwritten, and some felt a natural dissatisfaction with me, my faith in Christ, and what I was telling them. So now I had more patience and asked God for wisdom and love.

I remember one night we were together having dinner at their house. After dinner, Koula started asking me many impressive questions about God, philosophy, human rights, and social justice, and I saw how much she was interested in these issues. I was confused as to what to say, but I was encouraged by the Holy Spirit to share something simple and powerful from the Bible. I said to her, "Mrs. Koula, don't you know that God is love?" I felt that these few words began to work in her heart. That night at the dinner table, she received Christ after I told her about who Jesus is and how He can change our lives if we accept Him as our personal Savior. I remember her joy and laughter when I told her, "Tomorrow will be the first day of your new life," and she replied, "This night is the first day of my life!" It is a great blessing that Themis and Koula would walk with the Lord and confess their faith to everyone.

After finishing the day's work at Mr. Arvanitis's machine shop, I would go to Mr. Marangakis's restaurant and spend a few hours with them, helping them clean and close the restaurant at 11:00 p.m.

My main priority since I came to LA was to attend church meetings after work, which were held every Wednesday and Friday night and every Sunday morning and evening. What a great joy for believers to come together as one family, to worship God and to have fellowship with each other! The joy of new life overwhelmed me. I knew I was the happiest person in the world. Prayer and Bible study became the passion of my life. I had as my teachers Pastor Panos and the brothers Tsapatolis and Christidis. Pastor Panos was a preacher-evangelist with great passion and love for Christ. It was wonderful to see Pastor Panos preaching every week to the dozens of Greek sailors brought from the ships by Brother Marangakis. I always participated and shared my testimony with them. They liked to listen to me because I had the same experiences as a sailor on ships.

In early 1971, Mr. Arvanitis opened a store in downtown Los Angeles selling plastic flowers brought by his brother from Bogota, Colombia. In the 1960s and 1970s, plastic imported flowers entered the market and became very popular for home decoration. Mr. Arvanitis asked me to work half the day in the machine shop and the other half to create flower arrangements in the flower shop. I made nice arrangements with the plastic flowers and put them in the shop window for sale, something that caught the eyes of many customers. This operation lasted only five to six months because Chinese plastic flowers, with their great variety and very low prices, flooded the market and unfortunately, we had to close the flower shop.

My obligation to work for six months in Mr. Arvanitis's machine shop was over, and I decided to look for a job elsewhere. At that time, a Greek family suggested that I work with them in their restaurant, and I agreed. This small restaurant was run by a man and his wife, and I was the first employee they had. I worked there for about a year. After being laid off from this small restaurant, I was unemployed for three months, without the necessary money for my daily needs.

This period was very sad in my life. I thank God that a Christian American friend of mine, Bob, who was a chemical engineer, hosted me in his very small apartment. We had two couches to sleep on, and he paid all the bills and gave me some money for gasoline for my car as well. I knew that God sent him to help me, and above all, I learned to trust God, even in the saddened mental strain I was experiencing at the time.

For the next three months, however, I felt a dark cloud hang over me. I was afraid that God had abandoned me. I lost my joy and was not in the mood to tell anyone about Christ. I continued to go to church meetings, but I didn't feel the same as before. I was smiling on the outside, but inside I was crying with loneliness and fear. Thoughts were spinning in my mind again, and I wondered, *Did I do well coming to America?* I used to visit Greek restaurants in Inglewood city and meet other Greeks, but something inside me wouldn't let me talk about the hope we have in Christ. Deep down I felt that something good would come after this, but I didn't know what or when. I had stopped reading my Bible and praying. I didn't know why, but I didn't have the heart to do it, and I felt remorse for it. To my brothers and sisters in the congregation I had said nothing about the grief I was feeling at that time.

When I was working in the restaurant, I had gone to a technical college to become an air-conditioning technician. But when I lost my job, I didn't have enough money to continue the courses.

As I already mentioned, because I was unemployed, I couldn't afford to rent an apartment on my own, so I lived with my friend Bob, who was a very good Christian and always prayed for me. I still went to our Greek church in Los Angeles while he went to his American church called Bethel Tabernacle, which had about three hundred young people. They had two hours of worship each night and another hour of sermon by the pastor. Then, after praying, they went out into the streets, preaching the good news of the gospel. At that time, in the early '70s, a major revival had begun in California, resulting in the establishment of many churches, such as Calvary Chapel with Pastor Chuck Smith, Vineyard with John Wimber, Melodyland with Ralph Wilkerson, Chuck Swindall in the Whitter area, and Robert Schuller at the Crystal Cathedral. Many Christian radio and television ministries were also established. The Vietnam War was still going on and creating many political and social crises and upheavals. Thousands of young people protested the war and lived in communities as "hippies." At such times, people seek God, and He accepts them when they repent and believe with all their hearts, as it is written:

> And ye shall seek me, and find me, when ye
> shall search for me with all your heart. (Jeremiah
> 29:13 KJV)

One night I went with Bob to his church and met a young Greek girl who was happy with our acquaintance and asked me to pray for her father and mother because they were going through difficult times and were on the verge of divorce. One day I agreed to go to visit her parents in their apartment. When I got there, an ambulance was taking her father to a hospital for emergency care. The next day I went and visited him at the hospital. He had attempted suicide but survived, thank God! I told him about Jesus's love and prayed for him. I told him that his sins were paid for on Jesus's cross, that Christ wants us to live a holy life, and that He will give us the desire and ability to do so if we sincerely open our hearts. He understood what I was saying to him, and we prayed that he would accept Christ into his heart. He told me that his name is Koukouras and he was from the island of Rhodes. I never saw him again, but I heard that he was reunited with his wife after his recovery. Remember his name because that name will appear in my story nine years later in Rhodes.

My friend Bob encouraged me to apply to various jobs in my field as an engineer. By now my English had become better, and through night school I learned many new technical terms. So I prayed and started looking in the newspapers for ads for work in the fields of engineering. I drove down to the Port of Los Angeles and applied to three shipyards to work as an engineer.

Strange job application

I remember applying to the shipyard "California." I went to an office and was interviewed for an hour with many questions that were very strange. Some of them were the following: "How many minutes can you hold your breath? Could you stay in the small space of a barrel for two hours while doing calculations on an accounting machine? Can you ride a boat while you're lying down?" Then they checked my heart, lungs, and breathing. I thought it was funny, and I left smiling. I will tell you why later. On that same day I applied to the Bethlehem shipyard. They overhaul US Navy ships and wanted an engineer to repair parts from those ships. I spoke to the supervisor, Art Baker, a Christian, and he hired me immediately. He asked me to come and start the next day and told me that the company would provide me with all the tools I would need.

As I was leaving the shipyard, I stopped by the side of the road and thanked God for finding work. I asked him to forgive me for the doubts I had and the depression I felt. It was June 1972. This new job gave me a new professional direction in mechanical engineering and manufacturing, which would last until I retired.

SOMETHING VERY FUNNY

While I had been working in the shipyard for more than a month, I received a letter from the company that had given me that strange interview with the strange questions. They informed me that I had been hired at the California shipyard and they wanted me to be trained to operate small atomic submarines that surveyed the ocean depth between Los Angeles and Catalina Island, twenty-eight miles away in the Pacific Ocean. I burst into laughter because, when I applied to the California shipyard, I walked into the wrong building that was a government seabed mapping office. I had passed all the written and physical exams—as if I were Jacques Cousteau or Captain Nemo!

A few months later at our Greek church in Los Angeles, I met a young Greek man named George Pehlivanos, from Diavato, Veria, northern Greece. We became very good friends as we were united by a common faith in Jesus Christ. We were both on our own and decided to share an apartment for economy, of course with the agreement of my friend Bob. To this day, George and I consider each other dear friends. Finally, I had another Greek friend with whom I studied the Bible and prayed with, went to church together, and had accountability with each other. This did not last long, because in December 1973, he married a beautiful Greek woman from Pasadena, California: Margo. To this day we reminisce about the first days we were together and enjoyed our friendship and beautiful memories.

One of the greatest opportunities I had to learn to serve others was working with my pastor, Ernest Panos. We used to visit Greek restaurants (and there are many here in Los Angeles) and talk to them about the new life in Christ. I was confessing how Jesus changed my life and gave me a higher purpose, to live in His presence, which is the greatest joy of life. I learned so much from Pastor Panos over time. The greatest thing I learned from him was to seek humility and share the truth of my own experiences with Jesus, always with true love.

I now know that the greatest satisfaction a person can have is to love God with all your heart, soul, and mind and then confess it to others, starting with your family. The Bible in Matthew chapter 5, verses 15 and 16 says, "People do not light a lamp and put it under a basket but on a lampstand, and it gives light to all in the house. In the same way, let your light shine before people, so that they can see your good deeds and give honor to your Father in heaven" (NET). The light starts inside your own house first, then spreads to others. Never the opposite.

Pastor Panos—with much humility, love, and wisdom—spoke to strangers about God's love and Jesus Christ's sacrifice on the cross on Calvary. Brother Marangakis continued to drive Greek officers and sailors to church and then took them to Pastor Panos's house for dinner. Many times I went with Brother Marangakis when he took the sailors back to their ships. I was very happy that many of their questions about life, religion, God, and the New Testament could be answered.

My desire to serve the Lord grew day by day. I shared the gospel with many Greeks and Americans and served the elders of the congregation. I taught English to the Greek immigrants who had come from Katerini, Greece, to our church and Greek to the young people of our church, as I was in charge of the youth for a few years.

Mr. and Mrs. Valassi with our daughter, Jennifer

Among the immigrants, there was an elderly couple, Haralambos and Margarita Valassi. I considered them my parents and helped them since they did not know English or how to drive a car. I even found them a job and drove them when they weren't using the bus. We met their daughter, Betty Valassi, a few years later when she visited America with her husband, the actor Titos Vandis. Titos worked for many years as an actor in Hollywood, and we became friends. He also came to our church, and we gave him a Bible. Every time he visited us, we prayed together and studied God's Word. He told me that there were treasures in the Bible he had discovered and that he read it daily. His love for Christ was genuine, and he wasn't afraid to share his new faith with other actors in Hollywood. Mr. Vandis was an honest and straightforward man. From the beginning we became good friends.

Our good friends Betty Valassi, Titos Vandis, Nikos Menissalis,
with my wife and children in front of our house

IN RHODES, AS A CHANGED MAN (1973)

In early May 1973, I went to Rhodes to visit my relatives and give them my testimony of how Jesus Christ changed my life. I spoke to my parents, relatives, and neighbors. Some listened with joy and others with doubts. However, they all accepted my sincerity and love for them.

A great experience I had when I visited my old neighborhood in Rhodes, and it is worth telling you, was the liberation, with God's intervention, of a young girl from an evil spirit.

One day, walking near my house, I passed by the house of a cobbler, Stavros Nikolaidis. He was very old, almost blind from the cataract in his eyes, but even then he was repairing shoes. I came in to talk to him about the Lord and my experience with Jesus. He put down the shoes he was making, embraced me in tears, and told me that the Lord had sent me to him. He prayed that all Rhodians would become true Christians. He asked me to read to him from a New Testament he had there, and he said, "You are Peter the theologian." I hugged him with joy, while his old wife had doubts about my testimony and asked me many questions. Stavros asked me to stay another hour with him because the women of the area came to the store to pray. They called him "Saint Stavros."

Within half an hour, twelve to fifteen women of all ages entered the small room and, kneeling on the dirt floor, prayed the Lord's Prayer. Some wept, asking God to forgive their sins, and some prayed for their sick relatives. I prayed with them, next to Stavros. I noticed that a man was waiting outside the door. Stavros asked me to share something from the New Testament. So I spoke from John 3:16 while the women were crying and trying to kiss my hand, which made me very uncomfortable. After about an hour of prayer, Stavros asked everyone to get up and leave. "It is time to go home now," he said.

Then the man standing outside entered and, after kneeling, told Stavros, in broken Greek, about his daughter who had been possessed by an evil spirit for about three months. The man was Turkish and lived on a farm near the village of Trianta. He asked Stavros to go and pray for her. Then Stavros asked me to go and pray for her, while he stayed behind and prayed about it in his one-room shop, which was also his one-room house. I felt very uncomfortable going and I was a little scared because he asked me to go at 9:00 p.m. to the village that was seven kilometers away. His house was a five-minute walk from the main road, across some unlit fields in the area. Stavros told me to go and not be afraid because it was Jesus who sent me to the Turks.

AN INCOMPREHENSIBLE
EVENT THAT ENDS
WITH JOY

I went by bus and arrived in the village around 8:30 p.m. and walked in the direction he told me to reach his old farm. As I entered the house, I met his wife and eight to ten Turkish friends and relatives of the couple, who were all waiting for me to see what would happen. He told me to wait there until his daughter arrived, around 9:00 p.m. I felt God's Spirit guiding me to share my testimony and God's love with everyone in the room. I told them that many years ago when we lived there, a Turk had helped my family when there was an earthquake. I told them that God loves us and wants us to have a personal relationship with Him, so He sent His Son Jesus to die on the cross and forgive us of our sins. I remember asking them if they believed in Jesus, and some of them said yes. I even asked them if they believed in Jesus's resurrection. Only two people said yes. One was the girl's father, and they were waiting for her to come from work and see what would happen with me there to pray for her. Then I said to them, "I am here today to pray to Jesus Christ, who is alive in heaven, to deliver this girl from the evil spirit." Everyone agreed that she was possessed by an evil spirit. Her father told me to hide the Bible when the daughter entered the room. I told him, "No, I won't hide it from her because I'm not afraid."

Around 9:00 p.m., we heard her voice as she came home because she was talking to herself very loudly. She opened the door, walked in, and, seeing everyone in the room, asked why everyone was there. She was about twenty-two to twenty-five years old. She looked at her mother and father and then saw me. "We are here to pray for you so that Jesus can make you healthy again," I told her. That was all she heard, and she ran to her father and mother, kissed them with tears of joy, and then ran to everyone else, saying that she was already feeling very good! I prayed for each of them, and they all embraced me with joy. Then I left around 9:30 p.m., and the father followed me and tried to kiss my hands again and give me some money, but of course I refused to take it. He told me he was sure his daughter was healed. He told me that three months ago, she had gone wild and was beating everyone, even her parents. She attacked the village priest with words that took her parents by surprise. To what extent she was "possessed," I do not know.

A few days later, the father came to Stavros's shop to tell him that his daughter was a new person and behaved as she used to. The father told Stavros that he believes in the resurrection of Jesus Christ, especially since his daughter was healed. It's hard for me to understand what happened to this young girl, but all I know is that God definitely performed a miracle.

After forty-five days in Greece, I returned to America and continued to minister in our church while continuing to work at the shipyard. One of my best friends in those early years at the Los Angeles church was Peter Solomos. His parents were originally from Sparta, but he was born in the United States. He helped me in my Christian walk, explaining and analyzing deep spiritual truths of the Bible and, above all, the grace of God. It is amazing that fifty years later, we are talking on the phone about the same subject: the grace of God. God's grace is something we understand very little about. It is easier to understand God's judgment. But grace to a sinner is difficult for our human minds to understand. God gives grace as a gift based on His eternal love.

> For it is by grace you have been saved, through faith—and this is not from yourselves, it is the gift of God—not by works, so that no one can boast. (Ephesians 2:8–9 NIV)

GOD MADE US PARTNERS AND BEST FRIENDS FOR LIFE

In 1973 my friend Peter left our Greek church and went to an American church temporarily. He had a nice voice and sang in a big choir there. I felt very bad that he had left our church because I had learned so much from him and from his walk with God. I learned that God allows changes in our lives; we may not understand the reason at the moment, but later we see the spiritual benefit. We thank God for His infinite wisdom, His love, and His care for us and our future with Him; and we trust God who cares more about us than we do ourselves. My friend Peter met a beautiful American girl from a Christian family named Nancy. They fell in love immediately and planned their wedding for the following year. He asked me to be best man at his wedding. Peter and I started visiting his future wife's family. I was very impressed by how faithful this family was to God. They were the first American Christian family I had ever met. I had the impression that only Greeks could be good Christians but found out that my idea was incorrect and came to the conclusion that there are thousands of Christians around us we just have not met yet.

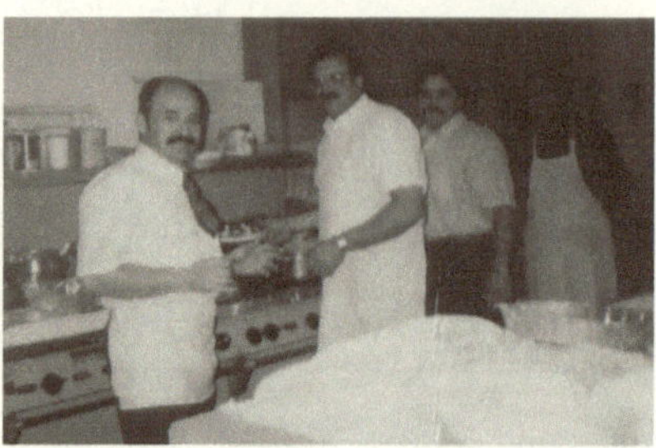

Peter Solomos, Chris Marangakis, Angelo Radoumis, and me

Peter and I often went to Nancy's family home. She wanted to learn some Greek phrases that she would say to her future Greek relatives on her wedding day. Nancy's older sister, Mary, participated in Greek lessons so that she, too, could say a few words at her sister's wedding to their Greek guests. Mary had just finished college and was starting teaching physics and chemistry classes in high school. As I taught the two young ladies in their dining room, I felt a little nervous because as I talked to Mary about my life in Greece and my family, I saw in her a gentle Christian spirit and saw the pure genuine joy in her eyes when she spoke with me. However, I was a little afraid that she might not like me after all. We exchanged thoughts about God, the Bible, the Christian life, and our future dreams. I never thought I would like an American young lady so much. As the days went by, I visited her at her home more often, and we talked about various topics related to her sister's wedding.

After Peter and Nancy's wedding, finally I took the courage to ask Mr. Forrest Ray, Mary's father, for permission to take his daughter out to dinner. He told me, "Peter, you have my blessing, but you have to ask her!" As we started dating, we exchanged thoughts on many topics and found that we agreed on everything—about God, about our purpose in life, about the responsibilities of man and woman, about family matters, about serving the Lord with all our hearts, about our ministry in the church, and about every other opportunity God would give us to serve Him in the future.

I was so impressed by her love for God and her respect for her parents and family values. So I began to pray to the Lord to see if this was His will for my life. The more I prayed, the more I loved her and dreamed of marrying a Christian girl like her. I never thought I would meet such a girl because I thought she existed only in my imagination.

I found that I was so comfortable talking with her parents because they showed so much interest in me and my family in Greece. I was impressed with Mary's father, who, in time, became a close friend and gave me a loving example of a husband and father to his family. He respected his wife and was always kind and tender to her, showing her a sensitive and strong love for her. I was also impressed with her mother, Barbara, who had a meek and humble spirit and yet was wise and intelligent and had a great knowledge of the Word of God and her quiet, joyful kindheartedness she always showed to me when I came over. She always asked me to stay for dinner, and her cooking was amazing. I'll never forget the second time I met Mrs. Barbara. She asked me by name about my sister Anastacia in Germany, my sister Tota on the island of Kos, and my brother George and sister Kathi on the island of Rhodes. That meant so much to me that somebody would remember my entire family by name and details about them after meeting me only once before. Mary's parents created in me a sense of trust for my future with them as a family. They were genuine people with Christ-like love.

As time went by, I met the rest of the Ray-Tanksley family, who were close to one hundred in number at their picnics where I met aunts and uncles and cousins who all embraced me with so much Christian love and respect.

When I took the liberty to ask her father for her hand in marriage, her parents accepted me with open arms and prayed for us. On December 21, 1974, we were married. We celebrated forty-eight years of marriage, in 2022. The years have passed so quickly and are filled with beautiful memories of service to God, to our family, and to everyone else God has brought into our lives. Very often I call my wife Mary "Proverbs 32." Because she surpassed the virtues of the perfect woman described by Solomon in Proverbs chapter 31.

Peter and Nancy, Mary and myself—both newlyweds

My dream of having a loving Christian wife, faithful children, and a happy home was fulfilled far beyond my expectations because God made it happen. I am so grateful to the Lord for His guidance and protection throughout life's journey. I worship Him, praise Him, and serve Him with inexpressible joy as pastor of the same church in which the Lord changed my life on the weekend of July 4, 1969.

Some time ago, I thought that if I had everything I wanted in my life (to be in America, to have a good job, family with a beautiful wife and children, to go on excursions, etc.), I would be the happiest person in the world and that nothing could change my mind. However, after experiencing in such a miraculous way the presence of Jesus Christ, the Son and Word of God, in my life, I realized that what makes man truly happy is not the acquisition of many material possessions but the worship and service of the Creator God in our lives. The most important thing in life is to have Jesus as your Lord and Savior and follow Him. All my dreams were true, but they were limited by human imagination in my mind. But when Jesus Christ came into my life, He gave me a new heart and new life with His Holy Spirit and opened my eyes to see the world from His perspective. God's love, which surpasses all knowledge, came true when I received Him into my heart and life. He changed my life forever.

There is no greater purpose in my life now than to share with others God's love, the meaning of Jesus's sacrifice on Calvary, and the miracle of His resurrection. The cross of Christ is no longer a religious symbol without any real meaning. There is no greater joy in a Christian's life than to see people accept this eternal truth when

God touches them, as He once touched me, and receive eternal life and the joy of knowing it.

The apostle John writes in third Epistle in verse 4: "I have no greater joy than this than to hear that my own children walk in the truth." So I appeal to anyone who reads these lines and is a father to pray for his children so that they can continue to walk in the truth. Jesus's words are true, for He is the Truth. The truth of the world changes from place to place and from day to day, but God's Truth was, is, and will always be the same. Jesus explicitly states of Himself: "I am the way, and the truth, and the life; no one comes unto the Father except through Me" (John 14:6).

In 1977 I felt called by God to attend a theological school in Anaheim, California. It was called the Melodyland School of Theology and was part of the Melodyland Church with thousands of members, added during the revival of the '70s. All my classes I took were in the evening because I worked in the shipyard during the day. I took courses on Bible history, Bible prophecy, apologetics, Christian doctrines, the relationship between the Old and New Testaments, prayer, ministry, church, and missions in the field. I had many professors, but the ones I remember most were Walter R. Martin (author of *Kingdom of the Cults*), Dr. Michael I. Esses (a former Jewish rabbi), and John Stewart.

The dean of the faculty was Dr. John Warwick Montgomery, who spoke Greek and Hebrew and was a humble servant of God. He held a law degree and a doctorate in apologetics and biblical theology. As a Christian lawyer, he defended Costas Macris at the Athens Court of Appeal, when he was unfortunately accused of proselytizing. Costas Macris was a Greek missionary in Papua New Guinea and had returned to Greece as an evangelist. Please read his biography entitled *If I Had Two Lives*. With these courses in the theology school, God increased my faith, and while I had many questions about the Bible and questions about many topics, God gave me the answers through these godly teachers.

Paul writes in his Epistle to the Ephesians: "He [God] gave some apostles, some prophets, some evangelists, others pastors and teachers, for the perfection of the saints, for the work of ministry, for the edification of the body of Christ; until, without exception, we all come to the unity of faith, and of the knowledge of the Son of God, into a perfect man, in measure of the age of the fullness of Christ" (4:11–13). The greatest thing I learned in these courses and in my fifty years of life in Christ was that there are many truly born-again believers in many different Christian churches around the world. I also learned that it is not the names of the various churches that matter to God, but the hearts of men and women who trust in Him and follow Him throughout their lives.

I had planned to finish theological school and get my degree, attending classes for two years, but unfortunately the Melodyland Church stopped operating after a major scandal. I was very discouraged about what had happened at the theological school, but I was greatly encouraged by God to continue with even more passion and the spiritual knowledge that He put in my heart. One of the professors at the school, Dr. Messer, gave all the couples in the school a test for character diagnosis. My wife and I took the test and answered thirty-nine questions about our relationship with the Lord, our relationship with each other, and with other people. We sat separately from each other while answering the questions. I was delighted when Dr. Messer said that my wife and I answered all the questions in exactly the same way, showing us how truly alike and equally yoked we are. Sometimes we both recall that test, and it is with great joy that we thank God for uniting us as a couple to serve Him throughout our lives.

In August 1977, my wife gave birth to our first daughter, Jennifer. Two years later, our son, John, was born. Then, three years later, our second daughter, Elizabeth, was born. Today, after many years of family life and my children's blessed relationship with God and with each other, I can repeat what the apostle John says in his third Epistle in verse 4: "I have no greater joy than this than to hear that my own children walk in the truth."

A MIRACLE OF SALVATION—THE STORY OF YIANNIS APOSTOLIS

In 1979 we had two children and lived in Orange County about forty-five kilometers from Los Angeles. For a short time, Pastor Kyriakides of the Apostolic Church of Katerini lived near us with his wife and their three children. Early one Sunday morning, he called us with an emergency request. He asked us if we could go to the city of Santa Monica, about forty miles away, to meet a young Greek, Yiannis Apostolis, who was very upset because he was facing serious problems in his life in America. In despair and depression, he called TBN Christian TV and asked for help. The channel's prayer manager had difficulty communicating with him, but he realized that he was Greek and needed help. So they found Mr. Kyriakides and he contacted me and asked us to visit Yiannis Apostolis. After giving me the relevant information and Yiannis's address, I went with my wife and children to the place where he worked. He was waiting for us outside with a small suitcase. I never knew that this would start a blessing for Yiannis, his family, his village, and the whole island of Chios in Greece.

Yiannis was a strong young man, with great courage, but he had fallen ill with pneumonia and had a high fever. He told us about many things that afflicted him, and while he prayed to God, he saw no change. His family with many children in Chios suffered financially, and Yiannis could not help them. So we all got in our car and went to our church. Pastor Panos's message that morning was intended for this spiritually thirsty man who, in the end, trusted Christ as his Savior with all his heart. How glad I was that a young man came to know Christ that day! After that, he would come to our house, and we would study the Bible together. Over the next two months, he never missed a church meeting, and many believers hosted him in their homes. After this time, he decided to return to Greece and live his new life in Christ with his family in Chios.

PREPARATION FOR THE TRIP TO RHODES (1980)

Pastor Panos, who prayed for our trip to Greece, always kind and good

Greece and all Greeks have a special place in our hearts. My wife and I always pray for Greece and the beautiful hospitable Greek people. My great concern is, and I pray for this, that all Greeks will become serious about the things of God and understand that Jesus Christ is beyond religion. A personal relationship with Jesus Christ is the proof of salvation through the changed life that follows. Jesus Christ is the Son of the living God, and He wants to have a personal relationship with every person in the world—yes, with you too. But for this relationship to be possible, the two members must agree with each other. God did His part and became man so that He could relate to mankind until death. He paid the debt of our sins on the cross and left the door open so that the second member of the agreement, the sinner, could do God's will. It is, therefore, man's free will to have a relationship with God. If man agrees, God gives him the faith to do so.

> For by grace ye are saved, by faith; and this
> is not from you; it is a gift of God; not by deeds,
> so as not to boast. For we are his creation, as we
> were built in Jesus Christ for good works which
> God prepared for us to walk in. (Ephesians
> 2:8–10)

Religion is passed on from parents to their children, but personal relationship with God is granted by our heavenly Father to whoever wants it. With this burden in our hearts—that is, that my relatives follow Jesus Christ, and after much prayer and the blessing of our church—together with my wife and two young small children, we went to Greece for a stay of six months. We stayed on the island of Rhodes and talked about this new relationship with God to all my relatives and neighbors. Some thought I changed religion, others called me a heretic, but I thank God for the few who believed and started reading the New Testament I gave them. Yes, a personal relationship with a living heavenly Father is possible. When this happens, unbelief gives way to faith, and the certainty of salvation drives away uncertainty and doubt. The saved man now abhors sin and seeks sanctification because God is holy.

Something worth mentioning here is that Mary, my wife, is faithful and devoted to God and to our marriage and supports me wherever God leads us, having a common purpose in our lives: to praise God in everything we do, to respect each other, to live in joy and peace with our family, and all together to trust God for the present and our future.

In Rhodes, we lived in my parents' apartment and slept in a bedroom with our two young children. This was our home for the next six months. The apartment was a bit small for six people, but we were content with what we had and we were all happy. However, after a week, I felt very sad because of my father, who smoked constantly in the house. My wife and children were not used to living in such an environment. When he continued to smoke and I told him to stop, he would get upset. He didn't like my change at all and was very disappointed that, as he said, "I changed religion." However, he was glad I had a beautiful wife and cute kids who loved their unshaven, smoky *papou* (grandfather).

Eventually, we decided to endure this situation, so my wife took the children daily outside to play in the fresh air. I tried to speak to him from the Bible on some verses that I had highlighted as important, but he did not think it right that I was highlighting verses in the "holy book." But he told me that he would listen to what my wife had to say because he felt she was a better Christian than I was. So Mary started talking to him daily from the Bible, and I acted as an interpreter. Many times he would leave his cigarette and go outside in tears, apparently because what he heard about Jesus's love moved him. My father liked it when Mary thanked him for raising his son well so that my Mary would have a good husband who loves his family. It was obvious that God was using my wife in sharing the truths of the Bible. My father was not religious; he never went to church because, as he said, he was very sinful.

Many times my mother, Eleni, while we were talking to my dad about God, interrupted us, saying, "Yiannakis, the children tell you the truth. The same is written in my New Testament, which I am reading every day. See our son now! He lives a clean life, God blessed him with a good family, he came and told us that God loves us. Where do you see the error? Believe me, Yiannakis, when we become like them, in our home, there will be no more cussing and fights. Aren't you proud of your son?"

My mother came to our wedding in 1974 in Los Angeles. She spent forty-five days with us and a few other Christian families. She came to church with us every Sunday. I remember that Pastor Panos invited her to church to pray so that she would have a safe journey back to Greece, and he also asked her to confess Christ as her Savior. We all prayed with her. From her heart and with tears in her eyes, she told us that she loves our church and all the Christians she has met because they helped her understand the Bible and God's love as she had never known it before. Since then, my mother read her Bible daily and methodically, confessed her faith to her neighbors, and finally joined the church that was later founded in Rhodes.

The first few weeks passed in Rhodes, and the fact that so many people did not want to hear about God and His love for them brought sadness to my heart. They told me they had religion and that was enough for them. When I told them that we can know right now that we have eternal life, they told me that no one knows if this is true. However, in his first Epistle, the apostle John assures us:

> These things have I written unto you that believe on the name of the Son of God; that ye may know that ye have eternal life, and that ye may believe on the name of the Son of God. (5:13 KJV)

True faith in Christ gives us the assurance that we have eternal life. How can we not rejoice at this fact?

MEETING WITH A SERVANT OF GOD

Brother Koukouras, my family, and my mother in Rhodes

Seeing that our plans in Rhodes were not progressing as expected, we were disappointed. Living in a cramped apartment and having two children who often fell ill, we remembered how comfortable our life in America was and thought about going back home. We started praying about it, and one day my sister-in-law, Dina, the wife of my brother George, came and told us that she had good news. She had gone to a glass shop and on all the walls there were inscriptions with Bible verses and the owner, Mr. Dinos Koukouras, told her that he was a Christian. Without wasting any time, I went to meet him along with my wife and children. After introducing ourselves, we hugged and thanked God for making this meeting possible. He told me that he began to truly believe a few months ago when he heard the good news of the Gospel from a soldier from Kavala, Dr. Lambis Sidiropoulos, who was serving at that time in Rhodes, and was born again. Meanwhile, when he heard my name, he told us, "I think I've heard that name before." Only a few minutes passed, and he suddenly rose from his desk, exclaiming, "You must be Filakouridis!" He hugged me and kissed me with great joy. My wife laughed at the lively way he expressed his joy. Mr. Koukouras had an event happen that morning before we arrived that made this rendezvous so amazing.

That morning, before we went to his shop, he had taken his cousin to the airport to return to America. His cousin had come to Rhodes to talk to him about the Lord and was very happy when he learned that he, Dinos Koukouras, had already believed and was saved. When Dinos asked how he met Christ in America, he told him that about nine years before, he was very ill and depressed because his marriage was in danger of falling apart and he had even tried to commit suicide himself. His daughter brought over a young man, whose name was Petros Filakouridis, to pray for him in the hospital, and on that very day, he accepted Christ as his Lord and Savior. This story brought tears to my eyes because the young man who went to the hospital was me and that after a simple prayer from my heart, the Lord healed a sick man, restored his family, and gave him new life in Christ. From that moment on, Dinos Koukouras and I became very good friends and started evangelizing the whole neighborhood every day, going to many other villages as well. Every night, we met at his home with his elderly mother for prayer and Bible study.

MISSION TO CHIOS

Brother Apostolis's family and his three-wheeled motorcycle

While we were in Rhodes, I went to see Yiannis Apostolis in Chios, as I had promised him the previous year. He had a job now, a growing family, and was developing in the grace and awareness of our Lord Jesus Christ. He had Bible studies at his home with friends and neighbors. He was very happy to see me and asked me to fast and pray that the Lord would bless the work we would do together in his village. So we started talking on the streets of Chios, in the market, in small groups of twenty to thirty people. By God's power, I told of my personal experience with God and proclaimed His love for all of us in Christ Jesus. I told them that we need to have a personal relationship with the risen Jesus Christ. A nun in the crowd shouted that what I was saying was right, but interrupted my message so many times that it distracted listeners. So Yiannis went and, taking her by the hand, removed her from the crowd. In the end, we gave New Testaments to anyone who wanted.

The next day, we went on Yiannis's strange three-wheeled motorcycle to his village in the mountains, about forty-five minutes away from the city. In the evening, we stayed at the house of a teacher

Yiannis knew. I continued to fast and pray when the next night I met his wife, Georgia, and their children. She had accepted the Lord and believed when Yiannis spoke to her of Christ. She was wise and kind, with much love and faith in Jesus Christ. Yiannis's father, an elderly and wise man, liked me very much and asked me many questions. In the evening, Yiannis took me to stay in the empty house of a priest who was a relative of his, and Yiannis stayed with his parents and family. I was hungry and trembling a little from fasting, but I felt deep down that something good was going to happen.

In the morning, Yiannis went to work in the city, and I was left alone at the priest's house without my Bible because I had forgotten it on Yiannis's motorcycle. I thought of searching the priest's small library for a Bible, but I couldn't find any, and that surprised me. Around ten that morning, I heard a commotion in the café across the street from his house. I opened the windows and saw a large Mercedes truck loaded with bales of hay for the cows and goats of the village. The driver angrily shouted at the villagers that he was paid to deliver the hay, but not to unload it. He demanded that someone go and unload the hay; otherwise, he would take it back to town. There in front of the truck stood some old people, but they could not lift anything. Most of the village young men were missing because they were sailors. I felt bad that the truck driver was shouting like crazy, arguing and cursing. Suddenly, I felt strength inside me and a voice urging me: "Unload the hay!" (This voice was well-known to me by now.)

So I resolutely got out of the priest's house and said to the driver, "Drive the truck around the village and I will unload."

"Who are you?" he asked me, puzzled.

"My name is Peter, and I am your friend," I told him.

Many old people asked me the same thing: "Who are you, and what are you doing in the priest's house?"

So he drove the truck to all the small stables on the mountain-side, and I was unloading hay for the goats and some cows. I didn't get tired at all. Instead, I laughed and cried, thanking the Lord for giving me the strength to do so. I told everyone that I was Yiannis's friend and I was waiting for him to come back from work.

When we finished, I went to Yiannis's parents' house, who had prepared food for me, but I told them that I would wait for Yiannis to come back so we could eat together. Women and men came to the house to thank me. I remember telling the truck driver as he was leaving that the Lord had sent me to this place to unload the truck and share with him the good news of the gospel of Christ. I told him that Jesus loved him and that he should be kind to the elderly men and women of the village.

Around 7:00 p.m., Yiannis came from work and brought me my Bible that I had forgotten on his motorcycle. Then we went out for evangelism, going to every house in the village. We told them about how Christ saved us and prayed for each of them. Georgia's sister, a young girl with special needs, received the Lord that night and told us to pray for her as we read for her from the Bible. The Christian witness and example of Yiannis and Georgia influenced her positively throughout the rest of her life. Her story would need another book to record. Now she is healthy and rejoices eternally in heaven, in the presence of her Lord and Savior Jesus Christ.

Today in Chios there is an apostolic church, thanks to the work and testimony of brother Yiannis Apostolis, his faithful wife Georgia, and his large family. We praise God, knowing that He works daily through simple and honest people around the world, manifesting His love as revealed by Jesus's sacrifice on the cross of Calvary. Years later, I learned from his son, who came and found me in Rhodes, that the driver of the hay truck believed in Christ and was born again.

RETURN TO RHODES

After my visit to Yiannis and Georgia Apostolis, I left Chios and went to Athens. I went down to the port of Piraeus to catch the ship to Rhodes when I saw twenty to thirty young men—Americans, Europeans, and Africans—gathered there, preaching the Gospel in English to the crowds of Greeks. The Greeks did not understand what they were saying, but the passion, enthusiasm, and kindness of the young people aroused their interest. I went and asked the person in charge if they were Christians, and he said yes. He also told me that they were members of the Youth with a Mission (YWAM) and had come to Athens to buy a ship that would be repaired at the Skaramagas shipyard and transformed it into a hospital ship that would travel to Africa and Asia. They would be preaching the Gospel and offering medical care free of charge to the forgotten and wounded world of poor people in the name of Christ. In my opinion, these are today's saints.

The ship was renamed *Anastasis*, which means "resurrection." The YWAM mission was based in Lebanon, France, and Cyprus. They told me that they needed an interpreter for the translation into Greek and that God sent me to them. They asked me to stand next to the Nigerian brother and translate his message into Greek because many people came to listen. I knew that God had prepared me when I preached in the streets of Chios for this very reason.

So, in Akti Miaouli, in Piraeus, between two large Greek churches, as the brother from Nigeria was preaching, I was translating into Greek, and everyone was listening to the Gospel of God's love, especially the Greeks. It was very difficult to understand his African accent in English, but I felt that God's Spirit was guiding the whole thing. To my surprise, I saw a Christian brother, a gospel worker, named Angelos Damaskinides. He came up to me and hugged me. He was distinguished by his humility and wisdom. After we finished, he continued the sermon in Greek, and I saw at that time a miracle taking place before my eyes. Many men and women knelt on the sidewalk and prayed to God for salvation. Tears flowed from their eyes and from our eyes because they made a commitment, beyond their religion, to their Savior, the Lord Jesus Christ.

I called my wife who was waiting for me in Rhodes and told her that I would be coming the next day. She told me that while I was away, there were riots in Rhodes. Protesters lit fires in the port and broke through the gates. The markets and shops were all closed and that they had no fresh food. Police helicopters monitored from the air, the government sent riot police into the streets, and no one could get out. So I bought two frozen chickens and put them in my suitcase in the hope that they would not spoil until I arrived in Rhodes. I invited Brother Damaskinides and some of the young people of YWAM to come to Rhodes the next week and talk to our relatives and neighbors.

When I arrived in Rhodes, the civil unrest had been resolved peacefully, but the soldiers were supervising the whole city. When Brother Damaskinides came to Rhodes, along with many young people, we set up loudspeakers with the permission of the local police in the center and in the castle of the old town. We gave out hundreds of New Testaments to the crowds who came and heard the gospel. I learned many things from this humble man of God, Brother Damaskinides. After his departure with the youth (YWAM), we continued outreaching every weekend to many villages.

YWAM—beautiful young men and women
who give their lives to share the gospel

Pastor Damaskinides and me

BACK TO AMERICA

Happy children in front of the Greek Church

The six months in Rhodes passed quickly, and we had to return to the United States to continue our ministry to the Greek church in Los Angeles. We left with broken hearts and tears, believing that God would bless the newly formed church so that it would grow spiritually and numerically. When we returned to California, I was greatly discouraged when I learned that the shipyard where I worked, my only source of income, had closed because union demands were too much for the company. I remember my mother-in-law telling me not to worry because the Lord had something better to provide for me and my family. So my sweet and wise mother-in-law prayed that I would find a new job.

Then I decided to go to night school and specialize in the aerospace industry, specializing in radars for airplanes. It was a bigger challenge for me and opened new doors for future employment. So I became an engineer specializing in building radar and other military equipment for Raytheon, Boeing, and Northrop Grumman. This new job was very interesting, which is why I remained in it until my retirement.

Upon our return from Rhodes, Pastor Panos and I began a new ministry of television and radio evangelistic messages in Greek, broadcasting in Florida, Chicago, New York, and Australia. Pastor Panos's son, George Panos—who did the filming, recording, and correspondence—coordinated with many radio and television programs day and night. He has faithfully served the Lord with all his heart, mind, and soul to this day for more than fifty years. He takes care of the distribution of cassettes and CDs, without any monetary reimbursement. He is a tireless minister, reliable counselor, and friend.

Pastor Panos and me—and my son, Yiannis Filakouridis

George and Elli Panos with their young daughter, Elizabeth

ORDINATION AS A MINISTER OF THE BIBLE

Servants of God must be ordained by the Holy Spirit, but earthly ordination is also important for approval by the local church as the body of Christ. Although I knew the Lord's guidance from the beginning, I knew it was important to be ordained and have the approval of my Christian brothers, who also had God's guidance. So in 1983, during the annual synod of the Greek churches in which many pastors participated, and after prayer, I was ordained by the United Fundamentalist Church, which cooperated with our Greek Apostolic Church. I thank God for the final approval and guidance from other ministers who are servants of Jesus Christ.

In 2003, we started another weekly ministry through the Greek newspapers of New York and Chicago, which circulated to thousands of Greek homes in the US and Canada. We have continued to write Christian articles every other week for twenty years in these newspapers, which circulate forty thousand copies a day. The relationship we have with newspaper managers in both Chicago and

New York is good. Readers call us free of charge, and we send them New Testaments, Christian calendars, and other Christian printed material. Everything is given for free, despite the high cost. By the grace of God, who opened this door to us, the good news of the gospel reaches many homes. Unfortunately, the Chicago newspaper *Diaspora* has ceased its circulation but continues its radio programs, which we participate in.

Brother Panos also began meetings at homes in Phoenix, Arizona. Pastor Panos went there once a month, and my family and I every other month. The city of Phoenix is about four hundred miles away, and I had to drive six to seven hours through the desert to reach the city. Sometimes, during the summer months, the temperature in the Arizona desert reaches 49 degrees Celsius (120 degrees Fahrenheit). We thank God for the safe trips we made for so many years since we never had a problem with the car, even though we always traveled with old cars.

A MIRACLE IN THE DESERT

In the course of time, God gave us another beautiful daughter. We continued our ministry visits to Phoenix. It is important to mention another miracle that happened in the middle of the Arizona desert while traveling. One day, after a strong urge, I put an extra can of gas in the back of the car, where the children were. My wife, knowing as the daughter of a firefighter the regulations and the danger of gasoline in the car, did not agree. But at my insistence and after wrapping the can with several plastic bags to limit the smell in case of a leak, we started our journey in the dry desert with the can of gasoline. I felt that maybe someone would need it on this trip.

I must say that I was discouraged about this long journey that we often made with my wife and three young children. After working all week, it was very tiring to drive seven hours through the desert. I asked the Lord if I should continue this work because, apart from being very tired, I did not see much increase in the number Greek believers in Phoenix. Now I know that we should never follow our feelings but only the guidance of God, answered through prayers. He is the One who opens and closes doors.

On this desert trip, God gave me the opportunity to express the weight I have always felt because I had not expressed my gratitude to that Turk who helped our family in 1957 in Rhodes, when that strong earthquake occurred and we were left homeless on the street. Do you remember this event at the beginning of my story?

We were driving through the Arizona desert on that hot summer day; we were about halfway through the desert when we saw a young man on the side of the road outside of his car waving his arms, asking for someone to stop. His car was parked on the side of the highway, so we stopped to see if we could help. No one else stopped for him. I remembered then, when we went out into the street after the earthquake that no one had stopped to help us, but one person did. We got out of the car and went to him to see what he needed. He asked us if we had extra gas. He had run out of gasoline in the middle of the desert. We said we had some spare gas to share, and he offered to pay for it, but we declined. I told him to take it as a gift from God.

After talking with him, I noticed that he spoke broken English with a heavy accent. We learned from him that he was in the United States for swimming training because he was going to participate in the upcoming Olympics. I asked about his accent, and he told me that he was a Turk who just came from Turkey for swimming competitions. I told him that I remember with gratitude a Turk years ago, when I was very young, who helped my family when a terrible earthquake hit our Greek island, Rhodes. No one had offered to help us or take us home, and we waited two days in the rain for help. I told him that this Turk came and took us to his house and that he let us stay with them.

Suddenly, the young man stopped me, saying that he would continue the story. So he told us about a Greek family with five children, who lived in his uncle's house. The man who helped us so many years ago was his uncle, who told them the story, and the young man remembered every detail! I hugged him and thanked him from the bottom of my heart for what his uncle had done for my family.

My eyes watered as my wife and three children witnessed this amazing event that we will never forget. How likely were we to meet the nephew of our Turkish benefactor in the middle of an American desert? After that, the weight of gratitude for the act of kindness so many years before was replaced by joy and relief I felt in my heart. We continued the journey to Phoenix, now knowing with joy that God is with us and that He approves of the work to spread His kingdom, no matter how tired we are or how long the journey is.

> And though the Lord give you the bread of adversity, and the water of affliction, yet shall not thy teachers be removed into a corner any more, but thine eyes shall see thy teachers: And thine ears shall hear a word behind thee, saying, This is the way, walk ye in it, when ye turn to the right hand, and when ye turn to the left. (Isaiah 30:20–21 KJV)

MIRACLE OF HEALING
FROM ASBESTOS

Unfortunately, my work for almost eight years in the shipyard caused me a serious health problem. My lungs were affected by inhaling asbestos microfibers. We had to remove the asbestos coating from the pumps, steam turbines, and valves from the ships to repair them. It was routine work, and it was not yet known how harmful asbestos microfibers were to one's health. We worked with this material without masks, and the dust entered directly into our lungs. Over time, I suffered from chronic bronchitis and sometimes pneumonia and had to take medication to treat asthma. I had medical examinations every three months, but the problem got worse. I coughed all the time, so I used an inhaler, along with various auxiliary drugs. Without medicines and an inhaler, I could not breathe. I was to use the inhaler every six hours, but I used it every hour or two. I always had an inhaler in my pocket, one in the car, and at church I had a spare.

Ten years later, after I stopped working at the shipyard, I visited a pulmonologist, and after many tests, he asked me if I had worked in a shipyard. I answered in the affirmative, and he told me that X-rays of my lungs showed an accumulation of asbestos microfibers and predicted that in another ten years, he would be treating me for mesothelioma, a form of lung cancer. I lived for many years in fear of this doctor's diagnosis.

I prayed to the Lord to heal me, but the disease worsened. The Lord listened to my prayers, but the time of healing was under His control. One evening when we had a church meeting with the youth group, they all went to the front of the church to pray. My children, my wife, and I were praying with them when my wife began to pray very fervently, expressing divine feelings as she had never expressed before. She experienced a special filling of the Holy Spirit, which was not just a feeling. I knew that something holy, sweet, and powerful from God had happened to my wife. After that, the whole church rejoiced and was blessed. At the end of the meeting, we got in the car to go home, and my wife continued to pray in tears as we traveled home. Arriving home, she preferred to continue praying in a private room while I put the children to bed. A little while later, I opened the door to the room she was praying in and felt a hot wind against my face. It felt like an oven. I asked her to pray for me, touching my chest.

The next morning, a special holy joy was pervasive in our family. It was my vacation week in August 1989. As we did every year, we put our luggage, tent, and all necessities in the car and went camping in the redwoods of northern California. We spent five days in the forest; went fishing; collected rocks; saw elk, deer, and bears; and lit a campfire every night. It was great! On the last day before we returned home, I suddenly remembered that I had forgotten to take my inhaler and medication. I had lived five days in the woods without medication or inhalation sprays. I was excited that I could breathe without medication. I was afraid that at some point, I would stop breathing. But my wife said to me, "You should rejoice because God has healed you." It was a miracle that I forgot that I needed my medication while we were at camp, but a bigger miracle is that I am now breathing like a healthy person.

When we got home, I went to my doctor for a new X-ray to compare it with the previous one. The doctor looked closely at both X-rays and, with obvious admiration in his voice, came to me and asked, "What happened?"

"Jesus healed me!" I said.

He, though a Jew, said, "Yes, I must agree. You are completely healed!" It's been forty-four years since then, and I've never had to use inhalers or medication. I breathe like a child, thanking God for my every breath.

ORDINATION AS PASTOR

Pastor Panos, Pastor Korkotselos, Pastor Angelis,
Pastor Kondilis, and Pastor Dr. Vourliotis

In April 2003, my pastor, Brother Panos, told first me and then the whole church that he had been instructed by God to ordain me as the new pastor of the church that I still shepherd to this day. In the years that followed, I have never felt stronger the blessing and special heavenly joy that God gives to those who serve Him.

In this life, we all experience many trials, some of which are very difficult. But God is faithful and never abandons us in times of need. Twenty years ago, I had a stroke, and God helped me make a full recovery. My precious wife contracted cancer and is now completely cured, naturally with God's help and the help of good doctors, medicines, and treatment. Every good thing is from God. All these and more events in our lives have taught us to rely on the Lord, to trust in His healing power, even in the darkest nights. Jesus is with every believer always, calming the waves of life's tempests with His Word.

Our children chose to follow Christ from an early age. They chose to marry faithful Christian husbands and wives and create godly families, following and serving Christ in their church and community, and for that, I thank God.

> For the earth shall be filled with the knowl
> edge of the glory of the Lord, as the waters cover
> the sea. (Habakkuk 2:14 KJV)

All creation manifests even now the glory of the Creator God, and yet many do not see it. The Bible is available to countless millions of people, and in it God's glory is revealed, yet many cannot see it there either. But when the Lord Jesus Christ, in Whom dwells all the fullness of God's glory, comes in glory, then the faithful people will say:

> Bless the Lord, O my soul: and all that is
> within me, bless his holy name. Bless the Lord,
> O my soul, and forget not all his benefits: Who
> forgiveth all thine iniquities; who healeth all thy
> diseases; Who redeemeth thy life from destruc
> tion; who crowneth thee with lovingkindness
> and tender mercies; Who satisfieth thy mouth
> with good things; so that thy youth is renewed
> like the eagle's. For as the heaven is high above
> the earth, so great is his mercy toward them that
> fear him. But the mercy of the Lord is from ever
> lasting to everlasting upon them that fear him,
> and his righteousness unto children's children.
> (Psalms 103:1–5, 11, 17 KJV)

Family photo

God sets the lonely in families, he leads out
the prisoners with singing. (Psalm 68:6a NIV)

To my wife, children, and grandchildren, I love you all—always.
I will see you again in a country where there will be no darkness,
no disease, no fear, no pain. A land full of joy that will always be
brightened by the light of our loving heavenly Father in His heavenly
kingdom.

The Lord is righteous in all his ways
and faithful in all he does.
The Lord is near to all who call on him,
to all who call on him in truth.
He fulfills the desires of those who fear him;
he hears their cry and saves them.
The Lord watches over all who love him. (Psalms 145: 17-20 NIV)

ACKNOWLEDGMENTS

I especially thank my brothers in the Lord—George Kantartzis, Andreas Fournaris, and Marianthi Koktsidou—and my wife, Maria, as well as all the brothers in the Lord who helped me write my testimony in a book in Greek and English. Without their encouragement and guidance, I would not have attempted this work.

AN INTERVIEW BY *VOICE OF THE GOSPEL* MAGAZINE IN MARCH 2022

(Founder of the magazine is Dr. Spiros Zodhiates)

It is our great pleasure to host in this celebratory issue Petros Filakouridis (P.F.), who, willingly, answered our questions. Although P.F. is not widely known in our country, because his multifaceted ecclesiastical and spiritual activities are mainly in America and especially in California, he nevertheless regularly and variously supports the work of churches in our country. You will see from his answers how adventurous and moving his life and return to Christ have been, which is of particular interest and shows the wonderful ways God uses to lead people, from different strata of society, to salvation. It would take an entire book to describe his life. In the interview he briefly mentions just a few important points. He is a man who loves Christ with fervour, and his ministry as pastor, for decades, in a Greek Apostolic Church in the U.S. is blessed. At the same time, it uses modern media to spread the Good News to thousands of our compatriots in the USA. His close collaborator and supporter in the ministry is his wife Maria. Here are the questions we asked of him and his answers to those questions.

Q: Describe briefly the first years of your life.

I was born in Cairo, Egypt to Greek parents who came from Kalymnos my father and from Samos my mother. In Egypt our family was well-off and we were happy, like most foreigners. We had many Greek friends. All five children of our family attended private schools and learned Greek, French and Arabic. My parents also spoke Italian. As a family we went to Cairo's Holy Trinity church. We were happy until the time came to learn from our experience that the joy and happiness that material prosperity gives are not permanent goods. In 1956 Nasser nationalized Egypt and expelled all foreigners to leave the country, confiscating all real estate and other assets they had. The only choice we had was either to become Egyptian citizens and stay or leave the country immediately. Without a second thought, we chose to leave and go to our beloved homeland, Greece. In Rhodes I continued my studies and graduated from the Merchant Marine Engineering School (Nireus) at the age of 19. I started traveling with the ships until I got the rank of 2nd Engineer on various ships. My dream since I was a little kid was to see America. I enjoyed seeing pictures in various magazines about the American way of life, but I didn't have anyone in the U.S. to invite me. So my dream remained a dream.

Q: What was the purpose of your move to the US?

The reason I immigrated to America was my deep desire and my irresistible dreams to come and see the amazing beauty of the mountains and oceans and to experience the freedom of people's lives, in the hope that one day I would participate in this dream. Also, as an engineer I wanted to expand my horizons in new technologies. Now I know, God had something incomparably better for me than the mere satisfaction of material achievements.

Q: When and how did you come to know Christ as your personal Savior?

I just liked America, without ever thinking about religious issues. I had no idea of God's providence and His love for us and for our eternal future. Eternity never crossed my mind because I didn't believe it. However, through the desire to come to America, God planned for something great to happen in my life, not because of America, but because of His providence that I did not know. So, I came by ship to America for the first time in my life in 1965 on Christmas Day. A middle-aged Greek man named Manolis Marangakis (Cretan) came to our ship to take some sailors with him to church on Christmas Day. Among them was an apprentice engineer, Petros Filakouridis! For the first time in my life I came face to face with the Love of God through these Christians of the Greek Apostolic Church of Los Angeles. A very different Church, because everyone showed love to us sailors unknown to them, and after the church dinner they invited us to their homes. Never in my life have I met strangers who would show us such love! A love that went beyond the simple human love I knew until then. How could this be the case? It was a question I carried in my mind for a few years, until God gave me the answer. I left by boat traveling around the world. It's a long story. I summarize it because of space. After four years I returned to America and met Mr. Marangakis, again who took me to the same church, where I met the same people, with the same Christian love. I was at a worship service on the evening of July 4, 1969, and the speaker unknown to me, Pastor Tingeridis, from the Greek Apostolic Church of San Francisco spoke of God's love for sinners. Every word of the message concerned me personally and passed from my ears to my heart, prompting me to repentance. As repentance did its work in my heart, my sense of guilt left me, giving way to joy and inexpressible peace and deliverance from sin. Without a second thought, I walked forward in the church with others to pray. My prayer at that time was a prayer of tears to God. When I got up, Christ was now a living reality very powerful within me, and the joy of my salvation could not be expressed in words. I was now a young person who loved and embraced everyone with unspeakable joy. I was born again!…as the Bible says. I felt young and clean! And that was just the beginning. What a wonderful God we have! I would not say that I knew Christ, but that He met me!

Q: How and when did you make the decision to dedicate yourself to
   the Lord and to the ministry of the gospel?

Immediately after the event of my joyful salvation, I began to
bear witness of my salvation to my neighbors, friends, and colleagues.
I returned back to my ship with a suitcase full of New Testaments
that I distributed to the crew and captain. I was happy because I did
the same thing that Brother Marangakis did five years ago. I began
to set aside daily time on the ship for prayer and to share with others
what I had read in the New Testament that day. Before long, while
I was still on board my ship, the U.S. Department of Justice invited
me to the U.S. as a technician and I received my visa and legal entry
into the country on November 1, 1970. My decision to dedicate my
life to preaching the gospel was not a decision of the moment, but
it was a steady, permanent, joyful extension of the love and joy that
God put into me, for teaching the New Testament, God's infallible
Word, and proclaiming the Love of Jesus Christ, all of which have
continued to be the daily joy of my life ever since. And because God
did not want me to live alone, on December 21, 1974, He gave me a
companion with the same heart, who always stands by me. We share
God's love. My wife, Maria, the love of my life, supports me, encour-
ages me and has the same visions with me. The Lord gave us three
children and nine grandchildren, all of whom follow God's way with
their Christian spouses. I could not imagine anything better than the
joy I have with my family in the arms of Christ.

Q: What were and are your ministries in God's work?

So naturally and unpretentiously does the Spirit of the Lord
guide us in our daily lives. In 1975 and 1976 I attended a theological
seminar with my wife. That period of time was a great blessing in my
life. I was taught by other American professors, filled with the Spirit,
the deep meanings of the Holy Scriptures. My faith deepened further, my dedication to Christ and His Word grew. God put teachers
in the church for our training. Since 2003 I have been pastor of the
Greek Apostolic Church of Los Angeles. Our church displays Greek

videos from local cable stations in Los Angeles, Chicago and Florida for Greek communities. Twice a month we publish a Christian message titled "Words of Life for You" in newspapers in New York and Chicago. With new technology in our church we can stream our worships live every Sunday, available online during the week because many of our members cannot come to church for health reasons. During the pandemic, for mid-week gatherings we use Zoom for members who cannot come. When the Lord opens a small door and prompts us to enter, we do so with joy. I also shepherd a small group of elderly neighbors, who meet every week and to whom I teach using my Greek Bible, which they want to learn with great interest.

Q: What are the challenges facing the Christian faith in our time?

The challenges Christians face in these difficult times are many. The Church faces the same challenges it faced in the first century, because the enemy of God and believers is Satan, who is trying to derail the Church from its mission. We can overcome challenges because we have God with us. We face challenges, especially now that they are increasing globally both in intensity and frequency, such as labor pains. Our Savior warned us of the end times. God wants us to focus on Him and the souls around us, lest we change our identity in Christ. Let us hear His voice: "Be faithful unto death…" (Rev. 2:11). The message he gave to the Church in Smyrna when Satan attacked her was to share this promise and encouragement with the churches that were being persecuted.

Q: Why is there so much confusion in the world today and how does this affect the Church of Christ?

The word "confusion" means pouring two liquids together. The confusion in the world is when worldly values are being mixed with Christianity where the people feel as if they fight to silence their consciences about the divine condemnation of sin and refuse to admit that creation is from God. They use as arguments irrational thoughts put forward by atheistic "scientific" communities. They are looking for a leader who will lead them to peace. They are willing to turn in any direction their leader would show them. The Bible exhorts us: "…Be vigilant! For your adversary, the devil, like a roaring lion, wanders around asking whom he will manage to devour…" (1 Peter 5:8–9). We are in the world but not in this world. We swim in a different direction.

Q: Do you think that some churches have lost their destination and are engaged in worldly affairs?

I don't have to believe it, because I see it. Christ told us that He has been given all authority in heaven and earth. He is always with us. He tells us to make disciples of our families, our communities, and the whole world (Matthew 28:18–20). We are able to do this because He has made His unchanging Word available to us, and He also gives us the Holy Ghost to guide us in our mission. If the Church makes compromises with the world at the expense of this eternal truth, the result will be the loss of this mission. If it creates its own unbiblical doctrines, then it inevitably goes in a different direction and will become a victim of the enemy's attack. Churches lose the guidance of the Holy Spirit when they aim for numerical growth and financial comfort, rather than the genuineness and holiness of believers. They lose their mission when they accept worldly doctrines, human glories, financial comforts, and their motivations are personal material gains. Do not forget, God endowed the Church with gifts (Eph. 4:11) for the guidance of believers, for the training of saints. The breath of the Holy Spirit will propel the sails of the Church to reach its destination. I am sure that God keeps us alive for a purpose. As believers in Christ, we are a precious instrument in God's hands to share the Good News of salvation with others, beginning in our own family and reaching to the ends of the world.

God loves you.

ABOUT THE AUTHOR

Peter Filakouridis was born in Cairo, Egypt. He was raised in a Greek community where, in school, he learned to speak Greek, French, and Arabic. When his family became refugees to Greece after political upheaval in that country, he had a hard life but was able to attend a polytechnic school at the early age of fifteen and graduated with a mechanical marine engineering degree at the age of nineteen. He traveled as an engineer with merchant ships all over the world for almost five years and saw so many different countries, but the one country he wanted to stay in was America. God spared his life many times, and in America he heard that God loves him for the first time in his life! After settling in Los Angeles, he went further in schooling to specialize in aerospace mechanical manufacturing. He found the love of his life, Mary, and they married in 1974. He began a passionate love for the Word of God and studied at Melodyland School of Theology for two years. He helped his pastor, Ernest Panos, to create a radio and TV ministry, and he began writing articles for the Greek newspapers in New York and Chicago. Peter and his wife, Mary, have three married children and nine grandchildren who all serve the Lord in their own church communities across the US. Today, he is the pastor of the Greek Apostolic Church of Los Angeles and has live broadcasts on YouTube and continues to write articles for the Greek newspaper in New York. He has retired from aerospace manufacturing but continues as a pastor and currently lives with his wife in Mission Viejo, California.